A Treasure Chest

KUMARI VERGHESE

ISBN 979-8-89043-975-8 (paperback)
ISBN 979-8-89043-976-5 (digital)

Christian Faith Publishing
832 Park Avenue
Meadville, PA 16335
www.christianfaithpublishing.com

Printed in the United States of America

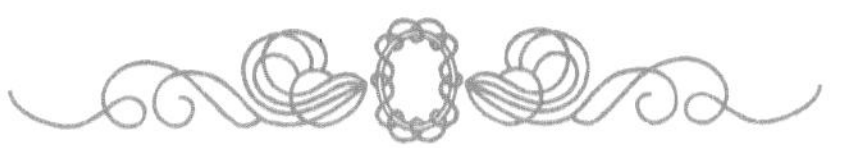

Contents

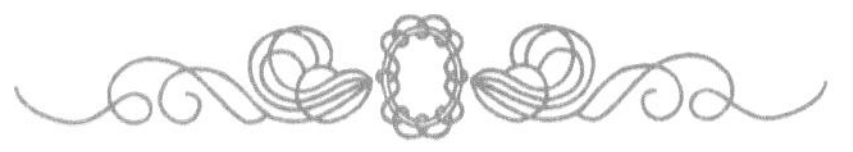

Preface

This book is a collection of random thoughts, sentiments, life lessons, and experiences from this journey called *life*.

I am indebted to so many people who inspired me to have the courage to take up this challenge:

First and foremost, my God who has been my source of strength, my way, my guide, my guardian angel, and my constant companion.

My beloved father, who had a way with words, a heart full of love, compassion, and unselfish generosity. His acceptance and pride in me led me to believe in myself.

My mother, who with her deep love, spirituality, and will of steel, told me, "Awww! Write, daughter, write! I love what you have written." She said that after reading the first few pages of the *Treasure Chest* that I wrote while on a trip home to Kerala, awake from jet lag, perched on a pillow next to her, typing away on the iPad, in faint night-light.

My classmates, who honored me at the fifty-year class reunion, as they selected several of my random writings to be included in the anniversary souvenir. Winning the first prize, an iPad Mini, for my amazing tapestry and their collective encouragement for me to write a book was a great honor.

My husband, who after our first brief meeting at my parents' home, told his mother to go ahead and plan our wedding. Though I did not wish to move to a faraway country, I believe it was God's will that set me off on this detour.

My precious children and grandchildren who taught me to love unconditionally, my friends, colleagues, mentors, church family, grandparents, cousins, various extended family, my patients and their families, all of whom showed me the true meaning of life and what really mattered. My cousin Sheela who said, "Ammamma, write, just write!"

A special shout-out to my son Tikku and daughter Tisha for loving me unconditionally despite all my imperfections and shortcomings. God had your back. And still has. And to my precious grandchildren and their dad, Anupam, who showed me that there is yet another kind of love that I never knew existed—one that is so pure, deep, and selfless.

A special note of gratitude to my daughter Tisha for showing me this path to make my dream come true. The story-worthy way to make writing this book happen.

To gather up some roses from the thorn bush along the way on this detour of a journey I started half a century ago.

And to wrap up some gifts of old memories and sentiments and gently place them in the treasure chest next to the bouquet of roses.

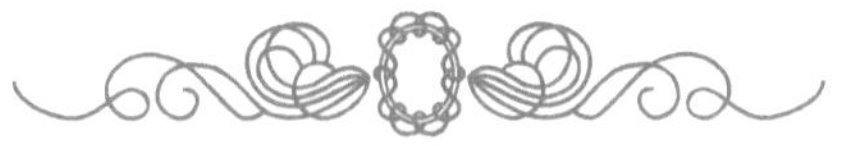

Parents: Angels on Earth

They love the thought of having you. They love you from conception. They wait for the day they can hold you in their arms. They smile the happiest smiles on seeing your face for the first time. They hold you, they cuddle you, they care for you with such tender care. Their lives will change forever from that moment on.

They hold you in their hearts. They think of you and pray for you with every breath. They provide for you and shelter you. They teach you by their words and deeds. They teach you right from wrong, they show you the way to godliness, they lead you back if you may go astray. They wipe your tears and ease your pain. They cheer you on and pick you up if you were to stumble and fall. Their hearts leap with joy with every triumph in your life and silently hurt for you with every bump in your way. They believe in you and wish only the best for you.

Then one day, they leave this earth. Your world seems dark and dreary. You feel that your world will never be the same. You miss their touch, their voice, their smiles. You miss the sparkle in their eyes as you want to share a happy moment. You miss the kind and loving smile of reassurance as you walk through a rough road. Your heart feels frozen with pain.

Then you begin to smile again. After the tears are shed and the goodbyes are said, you walk away. You walk away feeling grateful that they blessed you with lessons of a lifetime. You look in the mirror and see so much of them in you. You talk, you love, you live, you work, and be. You see a part of them in you in small and big ways. You smile again, knowing that they are always there.

Like the rays of the sun even on cloudy days. Like the fragrance of a rose that fills the air. Like the gentle breeze that brushes over you…

And you smile at the sunshine, look up, and say, "Thank you, God, for sending your angels who on earth I called parents."

March 4, 2016

Childhood to High School and Gems for My Treasure Chest

She left home at ten years old to fulfill her parents' plans for her—a better education—at a boarding school away from her hometown. The school was run by British missionaries and Orthodox nuns and teachers. With her little sister, eight years old, sick but eager to follow her, she held her tears and the pain of leaving home all to herself so she could be strong for her little sister.

She kept her heart and mind set on one goal: being a good little girl in every way possible to make her mom and dad proud of her. She prayed in the chapel not just during the routine prayer times that were part of the daily schedule, but also in the evenings after school, playtime, and bath time at dusk before study time. She had learned to sing and pray just as her grandmothers and her mother did. She knew that God was always there, watching her and leading her along the way.

She was kind to her classmates, just as she learned to be from watching her parents and grandparents, and just as she was to her three siblings. She knew to be good to her little sister's friends who looked up to her as if she was their big sister too since they, too, needed her to braid their hair as she sat by her sister and did hers after school during free time. After all, they didn't have a big sister with them at school like her sister did.

She set her heart on doing her best in class. She loved the sight of the endearing and encouraging smiles on her parents' faces when she brought home good grades. She wrote letters to her parents every week and told them all about her classes, her friends, her little sister, and how at times she was home sick but was doing fine (she didn't tell them that she cried frequently, asking them to pray hard that somehow they will come to school and take her back home and enroll her in a local school).

Her heart longed to be home too with her dear family, but she was happy that she was getting the experience of a lifetime. A life of discipline and structure, self-reliance through reliance on the one and only unchanging source of support—her faith in God—a faith that would prepare her for the many storms in life she would face. She learned the virtues and values of life: integrity, compassion, kindness to all, forgiveness, love, and admiration for all that is part of God's creation. She learned to love life with all its beauty and learned to see God's face in all that was around her—in all that was living and non-living. People, nature… she loved the beauty of God's creation and learned to respect all that was around her. Nothing felt bigger or smaller—all equal and unique.

Six years went by of hard work in school, staying among the top 5 in the class, short vacations at home, leaving home back to school, heartache of homesickness well hidden to keep it from her little sister…brokenhearted to be alone when her little sister decided not to return to boarding school after three years but determined to stay the course.

Graduation with first class was bittersweet—leaving the fine institution and the wonderful teachers, mentors, and friends was painful, but the joy of seeing the pride in the faces of loving parents and family was like feeling a cool summer breeze.

She can count the many gifts she collected over those wonderful six years, how she learned of God's grace as she watched a beggar woman with a toddler being chased away from taking a handful of dried wheat, possibly to feed her child, by a watchful maid servant by the door. How she knew that all that she enjoyed in life—wealthy parents, church family, excellent school, friends, family, beautiful home, beauty and wholeness—all of these and more were gifts from God, given to her by the grace of God.

Then and there she decided that she was only a steward of all her gifts, and she would try with all her being to be a good steward for the sake of that beggar woman and her hungry child—the first sight of God's face on this earth that she would see.

Wearing the uniform of a green skirt and white blouse, no makeup or jewelry, she knew that the girl who sat next to her in class was not any richer or poorer than her; all were the same—God's little people, serving His purpose.

Having an order and structure to the day gave her a sense of respect for time and people. Everyone had their time and their turn. Keeping time showed respect for each other, for in doing so, she was part of creating harmony in their little world. The rule breakers had to face consequences too, and she did not like public humiliation, which was what was in store in those days. She also enjoyed the feeling of being a good steward of time.

The free times after school offered unimaginable opportunities to explore herself. She made friends by sharing ideas, thoughts, and sentiments. She read voraciously while sitting under the trees, watching the sun set. Then she retreated to the chapel with her hymn book, sat on the cold marble floor, and sang quietly not to disturb other fellow silent worshippers. She prayed silently, thanking God for her blessings, asking for God's protection over her family, friends, those in need, and for herself too. She asked God for His guidance, then left quietly back to the dorm for study time, dinner, night worship with the group, and bedtime. Then the next day starts with a wake-up call at 5:30 a.m., followed by daily chores, morning prayer in the chapel, breakfast, study time, and all-day classes.

She remembers holidays at home with parents, siblings, and grandparents. A wonderful, enviable large home filled with love, laughter, family prayer times, and real times, visits from family and friends. Many family traditions around Christmases, Easters, and other special holidays, out-of-town vacation trips, just plain playing around at the home place with siblings, friends, and cousins. Oh! Those were the days!

She will tuck away these precious gifts in the treasure chest of her being and cherish them for the rest of her life. When life's ups and downs leave them hidden in the depths of her heart, she will reach in and take them one at a time, ever so gently, remembering the lessons learned in a faraway land in a distant time. She will dust them and polish them and with a thankful heart, reconnect with her source of strength and smile, knowing that He knows what is best.

******

She moves on from high school to college, carrying with her the gifts she collected, ready to face a whole new world. Little did she know then that the challenges she would face during the next ten years would pave the road for her entire life.

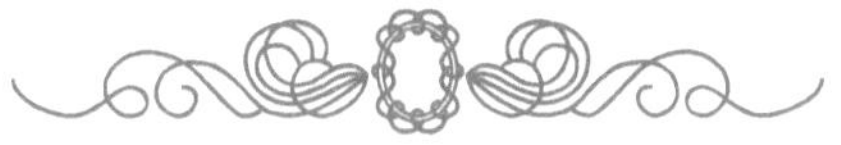

My Favorite Toys as a Child

Growing up in a close-knit family as the second of four siblings with many cousins, uncles, and aunts around, there was no shortage of playmates. Living in the southern Indian state of Kerala, we were blessed with ideal weather for outdoor play for most of the year. Toys were not a part of our play objects. We did have a few items that we enjoyed while confined to indoors during the heavy monsoons. Most of them involved "teaching activities" like blocks with parts of different pictures on all four sides. When put together, they would display a beautiful scenery, flowers, different animals, etc., much like modern-day puzzles with many pieces yielding various pictures.

We also had a "view master" and a pack of over a dozen discs. We would pop in a disc with tiny slides and look through the viewing glass. We would laugh in glee as we saw the beautiful objects each tiny slide would display. We traveled the world, visited museums and zoos and bird sanctuaries, all from the comfort of our home, taking turns with the view master.

There was another box with wooden blocks of different sizes and shapes that challenged our brains to build a house, a school, or whatever our imagination prompted us to.

Our sister had a beautiful doll wearing a pink dress with frills and lace, light in color with light brown hair. She would close her eyes if you laid her down and open them wide when you picked her up. For the most part, she just sat in a chair or was briefly held by our sister who preferred to play with her friends or us, her siblings.

Life in our small island village as a child during the '50s and '60s was so rich in its simplicity. Playing outdoors with siblings, friends, cousins, and relatives, taking walks to the river and the swinging bridge or to the lily pond to pick a few blooms, or trekking to the huge rock in the middle of the island to climb to the top and watch the sunset—these are memories that are etched in my heart forever. These took the place of modern-day inanimate toys.

There was so much fun in sitting together with my sister and girl friends, making garlands with fragrant freshly bloomed jasmine from our front yard. We used the stiff twine-like edge of a coconut palm leaf that made threading the flower stems through so much easier than using cotton threads.

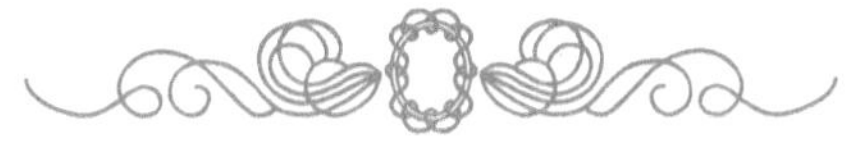

One of My Favorite Children's Stories

One of my favorite children's stories is from *Aesop's Fables*, "The Crow and the Peacock," where the crow stuck a few peacock feathers on itself. When other crows came to play with it, it chased them away, saying, "Go play with your own kind." Then it went to play with the peacocks, who mocked it and chased it, saying, "Go play with your own kind."

I always wanted and prayed for my children to be proud of who they are, to be and do their best, and to be authentic. I wish and pray the same for my grandchildren.

I consider my children and grandchildren to be the greatest God-given gifts to me.

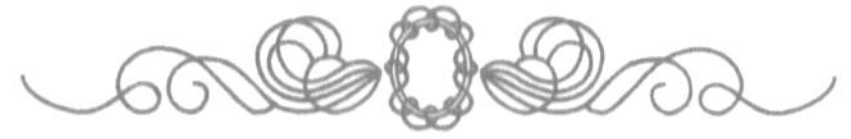

My Childhood Vacation Memories

Growing up in Kerala, India, which is referred to as "God's own country" by the Tourism Department, we did not need to leave our home state for vacation.

We would go to Trivandrum, the capital city, and stay at a five-star hotel, visit the zoo, museums, churches, temples, dams, and wrap up by visiting relatives.

Other attractions included visiting the wildlife sanctuary in Thekkady and driving to the southernmost point of India where three bodies of water merge—the Arabian Sea, Indian Ocean, and Bay of Bengal—called Kanyakumari, to watch the spectacular sunset and sunrise. Visiting families who lived by the famous backwaters of Kerala was the icing on the cake.

Spending summer vacations with grandparents and cousins brings back so many fond memories.

I revisit those childhood days through fond memories more often than I ever imagined.

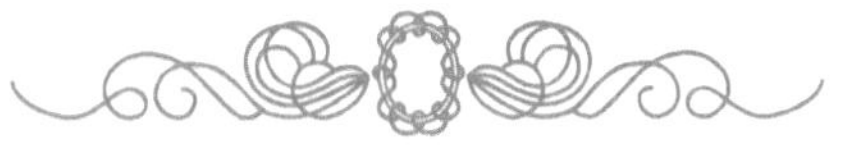

What Was I Like as a Teenager?

Terrible twos, teenager, empty nester—words that were not in my vocabulary until much later in my life in the USA, starting at age twenty-six. I had never heard those terms or understood their meaning.

But looking back, I wonder, what was I like during those years from age thirteen to nineteen? How did I feel or behave? How did others see me during that phase of life?

From age thirteen until age fifteen and a half, I was in high school, staying at an all-girls' boarding school. Life was very disciplined. Our daily routines were predetermined by the school management. We woke up in the early hours of the morning. Was there a bell? Maybe there was. We rolled up our mat, pillow, and sheet and put them neatly in the designated shelf, making sure they stayed tidy. If they didn't, the rule-breaker would receive a "black mark" on their score sheet. At the end of the semester, during assembly, names would be called of the notorious girls who earned these unflattering black marks for disobedience. In front of the whole school, the principal would carefully administer slaps with a light cane, in numbers equal to the number of black marks.

I never received any, but I do remember receiving three for taking the blame for my little sister for her sloppy mat offense. We shared the same identifier—us girls from different classes were grouped and assigned to one of the several groups named after flowers, like "Lotus," "Tulsi," "Jasmine," etc. We were both in the Tulsi group and had the number 17. "T17" was marked on all our belongings.

She didn't like all these rules and was frequently homesick. So after a year or two, she convinced our parents to pull her out of the boarding school and she returned home to attend a local school.

So what does this say about what I was like? Was I a passive, compliant, insecure teen who feared rejection? Or was I a responsible, considerate, industrious, loving young girl?

After high school, I moved on to college, farther away from home, to the capital city. I stayed in an all-girls' hostel, sharing a room with six other girls, and attended Women's College, a state university.

Upon completing the one-year pre-university courses, including languages, Indian and world history, and science, I joined the undergraduate course at Assumption College, Changanassery, Kerala, a Catholic all-girls college closer to home, and lived on campus.

I had always known that I wanted to be a doctor, so I majored in biology and chemistry. After completing the first year of the three-year course, I gained admission to Kasturba Medical College, Manipal, India.

Throughout the rest of my teenage years after leaving high school in 1963, around age fifteen and a half, life continued according to the predictable routines of college. Leaving home and family to live in different cities in Kerala or out of state for medical school, I had to be disciplined, responsible, and reliable. The spirituality I learned at a young age and nurtured throughout my life in Christian boarding schools and hostels gave me the strength I needed to cope with the challenges of everyday life.

Those very experiences also provided me with another skill and a true blessing—the blessing of friends who became almost like family. We remain friends for life, some from our preteen days and some throughout college.

So what was I like as a teenager? I believe we had a collective teenage phase. We were each other's support, keeping checks and balances on one another. We laughed, we cried, we explored the beach, watched movies, and participated in school activities like dancing, singing, and acting—all as a group.

Did we act out or have "attitudes"? I don't recall. I do remember some of us falling in puppy love, experiencing breakups, and enduring heartaches like we never imagined. But we got through it, grieving together and helping each other pick up and move on. A few even found their life partners while still in school.

These teenage bonds have been tested through time and distance. We have defied all odds and have been blessed to enjoy our friendships into our seventh decade. Sadly, three members of this group faced early mortality due to cancer. Their memories remain as vivid in our hearts as ever.

My Favorite Subjects in High School

Although I always knew and wanted to be a doctor, while in high school, the subject I liked the most was languages—Malayalam (my mother tongue) and English.

I loved reading novels, poems, books of famous quotations, and—believe it or not—looking through the *Oxford Dictionary* and learning new words.

I enjoyed writing long essays, short poems, and letters to loved ones. One of the perks of learning to write essays and speak in English was earning the favor of our boarding school principal, Ms. Brooksmith (I attended an all-girls Christian boarding school from grades 7 to 12).

Ms. Brooksmith would take a small group of girls who spoke good English (in her estimation) for an evening walk. Many times we would end up walking to a bridge over one of Kerala's many large rivers. We would all gather safely on the pedestrian side facing west and take in the beautiful Kerala sunset.

She would ask each of us to describe what we liked about the sunset. I loved talking about it, not just the spectacular sunset and the colorful skies but also the formidable river, the coconut palm-fringed river banks, the late evening river bathers, and the birds hurrying back to the safety of their nests—all of it.

These trips earned some of us girls different positions in the year's all-district arts and sports competition. Ms. Brooksmith chose me to be the key player in her "shadow play." I acted as a hunch-backed old lady standing by a well, waiting for someone to help me. A kind young woman came by and drew up a bucket of water for me.

I stood straight up and blessed her, and immediately gifts and pearls poured out of the empty bucket into her clay pot.

Seeing this, a young lady who was not kind at heart approached me, the hunchbacked old woman, and demanded, in greed, to be showered with gifts, pearls, and other riches. The old lady stood straight up again, shook her finger at the young woman, and poured the contents of the bucket into her clay pot. To her horror, the young woman watched as a stream of all things ugly—like sticks, thorns, stones, spiders, and scorpions—poured out. She ran away screaming in despair.

All of this was acted out behind a sheer curtain, without sound or words, seen by the audience as shadows of us playing out our roles. It was an honor.

There were others who sang, danced, and played tennis. At the end of the District Youth Festival Competition, our school took home the trophy for first place.

This experience groomed me to take part in many extracurricular activities throughout college, medical school, and even during later years in the practice of medicine.

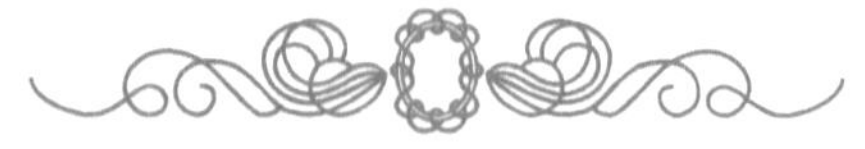

My Friend from Grade School and Beyond

We met in seventh grade, in June of 1959. Lizzy had just turned twelve, and I was six months short of twelve. Away from home, at an all-girls' Christian boarding school. Our homes were not too far apart, on either shore of the River Pamba. We had never met before but quickly became friends in no time, knowing that we were neighbors. Our younger sisters were in the same school too.

For the next five years, we shared the amazing experience of boarding-school life. We had to adapt to wearing school uniforms: a green skirt and white blouse, no makeup or jewelry. We lived, learned, played, and prayed together, along with a few hundred other girls from sixth through elventh grades.

As I had mentioned in my previous story, life at the boarding school had a significant impact. After graduating from high school, Lizzy and I joined an all-girls' government college in Trivandrum, the capital city of Kerala. Lizzy stayed at the large women's hostel while I stayed at a nearby small private hostel run by CSI (Church of South India) nuns. It was another impactful phase of life with deep spiritual guidance.

We didn't have any classes together but kept in touch mostly after school. Trivandrum was over three hours away by bus from our hometowns, so we would either ride the bus or train together during holidays and school breaks, back and forth. At the end of that one year of pre-university course, in May 1964, we parted ways to pursue "real college."

We both chose Medicine as our field of profession. Although we attended medical colleges outside of our state, Kerala, Lizzy in

Banaras and I in Mysore State, we kept up through letters throughout our college years.

Then, by sheer chance, we both got married in arranged marriages to guys who lived in the USA. Her husband, Bobby, in Washington, DC; and my husband, Babuji, in Chicago, Illinois. Lizzy and Bobby on September 10, '72, and Babuji and I on September 21, '72.

Babuji had a three-month vacation before starting a new job in Detroit, Michigan, so we had a long three months together (I took a break from the yearlong mandatory internship) while Bobby left for the USA a few days after their wedding.

Lizzy completed her internship three months earlier, got her visa, and joined Bobby, who by then, by chance, had gotten a job in Rochester, Michigan.

So after completing my internship and getting my visa, when I came to the USA in November '73. Lizzy and I got to pick up our friendship in person, in a faraway land just less than an hour's drive away.

From Detroit and Rochester, Michigan, to Florida and North Carolina, as wives, mothers, grandmothers, residents, fellows, attendings, and retirees, we've been blessed to share our lives (with all its joys, trials, laughter, and tears) in this adopted land for almost half a century. It's been a true blessing of a lifetime.

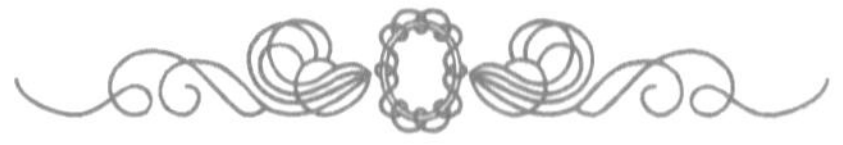

College Days and More Gems
for the Treasure Chest

Crossroads

From the sheltered life in an all-girls Christian boarding school just a few miles from home, with weekend visits from family and three breaks throughout the year, to an all-women's college in the capital city hours away from home, it seemed a bit intimidating. Having a great friend, neighbor, and fellow schoolmate, also starting the first year of college at the same institution, to share the three-hour train ride eased the anxiety.

Our 1963 preuniversity class, a yearlong transition course from high school prior to entering a bachelor's course or preprofessional class (if one chose to go into medicine or engineering), was too large. We were divided into several groups, each with around one hundred sixteen-year-olds. Half of us attended morning classes, and the other half attended afternoon classes.

Staying at a private women's hostel, run by a nun sister named Chechamma from the Church of South India, was an unforgettable experience. Her serene face, devoid of any makeup, simple all-white attire, no jewelry except for a wooden cross on a black thread hanging around her neck, her sweet smile, and soft voice left an indelible impression in my memory. Everything about that life offered great life lessons. Sharing a room with five other girls, all strangers from different parts of the state, with different family backgrounds and upbringings, we learned to get along, accommodate different schedules, and respect personal preferences.

The morning prayer and devotional in the small, pristine chapel, led by Sister Chechamma, set the stage for a calm and positive day ahead.

On one November morning, we went for the morning prayer with heavy hearts, having heard the dreadful news about the assassination of our favorite US president - President John F. Kennedy. Many of us cried, and we prayed for his soul, his family, especially his beautiful little daughter, adorable son, and his wife, as well as for his country. We went on to our classes and, between chemistry and physics, Indian and world history, English and biology, we snuck a little break to talk in disbelief about how someone could do such a thing as to put a bullet in someone's heart.

Long train rides back home during term breaks were fun. We talked about our dreams and aspirations, sang together, read alone, or simply gazed out the window and took in the breathtaking beauty of Kerala's rich, lush green paddy fields, coconut palms, colorful flowers, and vegetation. We were awed by the sunsets, sunrises, and even full moons during late rides.

Once homelife felt incredibly peaceful and joyful. The amazing love of so many people - grandparents, parents, siblings, relatives, and friends who visited, as well as the neighbors and church family - all added to the joy of being home. Memories of family prayer times at dusk and dawn, family meals around the large dining table, and sitting outdoors with family after sundown, enjoying the breeze and often inhaling the delicate fragrance of freshly blooming jasmine from the two vines that adorned the arch at the gate, are etched in my heart forever.

The household helpers were so much a part of the family too. Maria, whom the elders called by her name but the youngsters referred to as Maria Chedathy (due to her age, we were respectfully supposed to call her *Chedathy*, meaning "older sister"), had been there since way back when. She pretty much walked around and supervised other helpers, and sometimes got into minor trouble with Grandfather. He would catch her tiptoeing out of his room with her hands clasped behind her back, and he would ask, "Maria, did you take some of my chewing tobacco?" Sheepishly, she would smile and mutter something under her breath, which to this day I am not sure whether it was a yes or no. No one, including herself, knew how old she was. When asked her age, she would respond, "My mother said I knew how to count when the flood of '99 came around. You can count."

Looking back, I think Maria might have had a part in my decision to go into Medicine. I was impressed with my parents' and grandparents' spirituality and graciousness towards people in need. I knew I also wanted to "serve" people and "serve God." I thought being a doctor would meet both needs.

But it was Maria's tobacco-stained, random teeth and hearty smile that sealed the deal.

Maria, though as old as time, was quite healthy except for her frequent complaints of bloating. We, the kids, were required to take a vitamin B complex capsule every morning. I had nothing against it except that I didn't like the "aftertaste" if it came back as a burp sometimes. So, I had a vested interest in sneakily giving away my share every time. When Maria would complain about her bloating, I would take her aside, making sure no one was looking, and give her one of those capsules. Within a few minutes, she would return, pull up her tunic top to just expose her belly, pat it proudly, and say, "Look! It worked! That was good medicine!" It was our secret until at 10 years of age, I went away to boarding school. Then she would ask my mother if she had any of that medicine that I used to give her. My mother had no clue. When I came home on school breaks, she would ask, and being older and having more sense about honesty and truthfulness, I had to let everyone in on our secret!

But that innocent smile and blind faith in a little girl's quack medicine made me realize that helping is a two-way street. The giver and receiver both enjoy the fruit of the deed. The placebo effect helped ease her discomfort, and her relief and smile warmed my heart! So that was it. Doctor, it had to be - easing the pain, seeing the smile, smiling along.

A year went by, and preuniversity was done. Standing at the crossroads, it was time to pick a path: premed or bachelor's. The competition was high for premed that year, so I took the path to a BS in chemistry and biology with a plan to apply for medicine after obtaining the BS degree. Going to a Catholic all-girls college and staying at a ladies' hostel run by Catholic nuns was another eye-opener. The discipline, dedication, and commitment of those sisters were unlike anything I had ever imagined. On one of our intimate conversation times during the first semester break, I shared with my mother, "I want to be a Nun." She responded, "But I thought you always wanted to be a doctor. But a nun now? Why?" I told her I wanted to serve God like those nuns did. What she said in response will stick with me as long as I live. "You don't have to be a nun to serve God. You can serve God by serving His children. We can serve God in everything we do if we choose to put God first." Then she continued, "And besides, we are Mar Thomites. Our denomination does not have nuns anyway."

She wasted no time telling my father, who decided it was time to look at private medical schools. At the end of the first year of the three-year BS program, he had located the school, paid the entrance fee, and had me complete the application and attend the entrance interview. Thus began the amazing journey that started in June 1965 at one of India's best medical colleges—KMC, Kasturba Medical College, Manipal, India.

Friends After All the Years

About seven of us from the SSLC (Secondary School Leaving Certificate) class of '63 are in frequent contact via WhatsApp. Three of the seven (including myself) are physicians in the USA and have been here since the early '70s and are US citizens. My friend Lizzy is an internist in Florida, and I am a psychiatrist in North Carolina. Shoba is an anesthesiologist practicing in Philadelphia.

The story below provides a small narrative of life and the lessons learned from boarding school life from sixth to eleventh grade, although Lizzy and I joined in seventh grade.

Reflections of Life at Balikamatom

It was June of 1959 at Balikamatom Girls High School in Thirumoolapuram, Thiruvalla, Kerala. Two little girls from Edanad, a beautiful small island village surrounded on all four sides by the Pamba River, were entrusted to the care of a respected Kochamma of the administrative team. As they said goodbye to their beloved family, little did they know that they were in for the experience of a lifetime.

The younger of the two was nine years old and would go to the kindergarten side of the school, while the older one (myself) was eleven and a half. As the initial excitement of going to a boarding school with my big sister gave way to intense sadness and homesickness, those little arms tugged at my heart, and my eyes welled up with tears.

That moment in time taught me a profound lesson that would shape the way I related to others, especially people who looked up to me. My heart ached too, knowing that it would be a few weeks before we would go home again. But at that moment, I had to be brave for my sister, fighting back my own tears. I told her that we have each other, we will see each other every day, and that we will have lots of friends and it will be fun.

The character-forming experiences over the next five years laid the foundation for the person I would become. And for that, I have many to thank—Almighty God, who gave the foresight and discernment to my loving parents to choose this school, the founders, principal, all the teachers and other staff, and my fellow students.

Every element of each day spent at the school played a role in shaping my character - starting with putting my younger sister's concern over mine, which helped me understand the basics of empathy and compassion. The daily routine of early morning wake-up time, sharing the facilities with many other girls for morning chores, being on time for chapel, breakfast, and study time taught me to be good at time management.

Each chore in itself was a lesson in discipline—rolling the mat, pillow, and sheet and neatly tucking them in the shelf, avoiding the risk of getting a black mark for sloppiness. Skillfully using the limited time and shared space to complete morning routines and being ready to get to the chapel.

The amazing experience of worshiping together at dawn and dusk, and alone in the evenings, shaped my spiritual life. I cherish the memories of being in that chapel. I especially go back to that little girl in a green and white skirt and blouse with a veil covering her head, silently singing favorite hymns and saying prayers ardently, in times of struggles.

Watching our beloved Ms. Brooks Smith, all the kochammas, the sisters, and all the support staff carry on their roles with such dedication and commitment was so inspiring. The simplicity of life, from sleeping on a mat on a hard floor to makeup and ornament-free attire in uniform, simple but nutritious meals served on a basic plain steel plate with our initials that we brought from home, being responsible for cleaning it and putting it away after each meal—all these helped to develop priorities that mattered.

I learned that faith in God mattered, empathy mattered, humility mattered, self-discipline and self-reliance mattered, respect, attitude of gratitude, and servitude mattered. These, above all else, have helped me in all the roles I had to play since graduating SSLC (Secondary School Leaving Certification = high school) with first class in 1963.

After PUC (preuniversity course) at Women's College, Trivandrum, and the first year of BSc at Assumption College, Changanacherry, I joined Kasturba Medical College, Manipal. Upon finishing medical school and house surgency in September of 1972, I got married to my husband, a biochemist working in Chicago, Illinois, USA. Since joining him in November '73 upon getting the visa, we lived our first seven years in Michigan. We were blessed with our son in '74 and our daughter in '79. When I finished my residency in psychiatry and fellowship in child psychiatry, our family of four moved to sunny North Carolina in June 1980 to get away from the brutal Michigan winters.

We have been here ever since.

The life lessons I learned at the school and home prepared me to be the daughter, wife, daughter-in-law, sister-in-law, mother, grandmother, mother-in-law, friend, and all that I am. Leaving beloved family and home and making a home in this adoptive land, while going through residency, raising children, and juggling various roles, was challenging but was made easier by the pure grace of God and the resilience learned at our school.

Now, at age seventy-three, I look back and marvel with utmost gratitude at the providence of God Almighty, who has blessed me so abundantly.

That eleven-year-old little girl who went on to become a physician, a psychiatrist who held many leadership roles, practiced for forty-six years, and is now retired this year, only due to COVID precautions.

On a more personal and sentimental note, I cherish the memories of numerous hours of girl talks, silly jokes, and naughty things, like the time when there was a lot of talk about the end of the world.

One day, while we were at evening study time, a dog rubbed against the leg of a girl, she screamed, and all the girls from all over the classrooms jumped up on top of the desks and screamed and screamed until "Madamma" came around asking, "Girls! Girls! What is going on?"

No one knew why we were screaming, except possibly we thought the first screamer might have felt something like the end of the world everyone was talking about. None of us knew why or how the entire school of girls ended up on top of the desks as if desk tops would protect us from the calamity.

As she calmed us down and walked away, fear gave way to relief and our collective hushed giggles.

And the Saturday evening assembly in the large hall where we all met to learn proper English, as Madam desperately tried to teach us to pronounce *water* with only one *t* (and not the emphatic double *t*), saying *w* that sounded more like *wh* (and not the flat *w* as in Malayalam South).

And all the evenings where we played on the playground, or sat under the tree with a favorite book (as this one here who didn't much care for physical activities), or sat in groups and shared our thoughts, feelings, and dreams.

To the younger generation—take it all in, every thread of it, weave it into the fabric of your being… you will thank the day you stepped in through those beautiful gates and walked out into the world having tasted and been nourished by the best of experiences for a lifetime.

May God bless you to see the best and take the best even from tough and not-so-seemingly good experiences.

Thank you, Balikamatom School, and Ms. Brooke Smith, Achamma Kochamma, Atthukutty Kochamma, Annamma Kochamma, Mariamma Kochamma, Rosamma Kochamma, Appu Kochamma, Deenamma Kochamma, Lilly Kochamma, PV Varghese Sir, Pappi Sir, Sarah Sister, Maria Sister, Chechi, and all others.

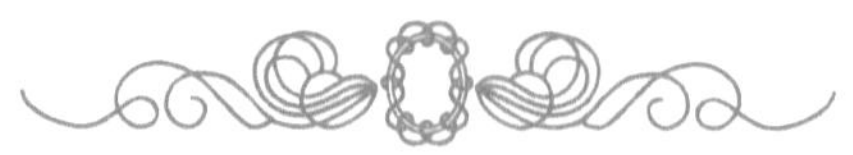

Do I Believe in a Higher Power?

Being raised in a Christian family is one of the greatest gifts I cherish. Memories of family prayer times at dawn and dusk, attending Sunday school with siblings, listening to my mother and grandmother hum Christian hymns as they went about their chores, and my grandfather saying prayers as he started the day are etched in my heart forever. The faith instilled in me through these experiences at a very young age took on a life of its own when I left home at eleven years of age to continue my education in an all-girls Christian boarding school.

One incident during the early days of school would lay the foundation for my personal faith journey. I call this "the first time I met God and the lesson He taught me about His grace."

As I was returning from the dining room to the dorm after lunch, I saw a very thin, scantily clothed young lady, a beggar, with a toddler girl in tattered clothes on her hip. She reached down and took a handful of the boiled wheat drying on a mat in the sun. A kitchen worker spotted her and shooed her off. She dropped the wheat as she walked away in shame, guilt, fear, and sadness, knowing that her child may go hungry until she could find some other way to get food.

As I climbed the steps to the dorm, those two faces haunted me. The pain and despair in their eyes were so piercing. I reached the bathroom on the top of the stairs, closed the door, and cried, feeling helpless that I couldn't do anything to ease their pain. I also wondered how and why I was so fortunate to be living a privileged life. At eleven years of age, I couldn't recall doing anything big or good to deserve all that I was enjoying. I didn't feel any different from that young lady or her child. We were all people, yet I had everything and they had nothing. I felt ashamed, sad, and angry that I was helpless.

And to the many *why*s I asked during the quiet moments of meditation at the school's chapel that I generously used during my free time, I received an answer. "Not by my merits, but by the grace of God, I am blessed to be a blessing."

I would carry that profound insight with me throughout the rest of my life. As I pursued my dream and passion of a career in Medicine, it helped me remain grounded and humble. In the face of many challenges while living in a faraway land and dealing with various struggles, I remembered those encounters where I met God face to face and found solace in the gift of His grace.

While God is omnipotent and omnipresent, places of worship stood out as symbols and reminders of the truth of His mighty power, grace, love, and protection. I am forever grateful to have belonged to the church family of my childhood home, where many of us, including my daughter, were baptized, many were married, and many of my ancestors are buried. I cherish the memories of our school chapel, which offered me countless quiet and serene hours to pray, silently sing, and contemplate the various realities of life. Now, in this adoptive land, I have found a local church whose motto is "all are welcome," and I feel incredibly blessed to serve as a lay Eucharistic Minister there, and to have had my three grandchildren baptized there. It is a joy and a privilege to experience the fullness of God's grace once again.

My heart sings with joy and gratitude as I remember the lesson I learned about the transformative power of grace at the receiving end. Instead of becoming cynical about the inequalities in society, I have used the blessing of grace to serve God by serving His people. I am grateful for my family, my teachers, and my mentors who showed me the way. The school chapel where I spent many quiet evenings praying for the less fortunate, thanking God for His grace, and seeking His guidance has always been a beacon of light in my faith life. The church our family has attended for generations, where many were baptized, had their first communions, got married, and were laid to rest, holds a special place in my heart.

The church I have been worshipping at for the last several years here in North Carolina, and where I have been blessed to serve as a lay Eucharistic minister, has been a blessing to my family. All three of my grandchildren were baptized there. It was a humbling experience to hear the church choir sing a hymn I wrote for them, combining two of my favorite psalms - Psalms 23 and 121.

The higher power I believe in, my God and my Redeemer, my friend, guide, and anchor, and the beacon of light, is Jesus Christ.

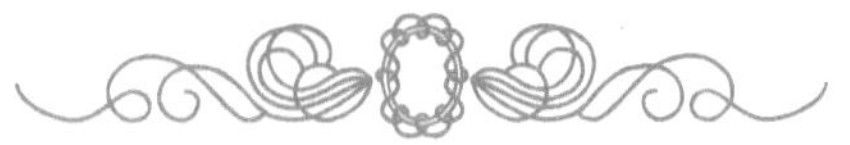

Am I More Like My Father or My Mother?

I love, admire, respect, and cherish my parents for all that they have been to us, their four children, as well as our entire families, extended families, church, and community. I learned life's core values by watching them, as their actions spoke louder than their words. They lived their values, and I observed and learned from them.

There are aspects of my life where I feel I am more like one parent or the other, yet it is challenging to define if I am more like one or the other. They were both incredible individuals, each with deep spirituality, integrity, kindness, amazing work ethics, generosity, and profound love for each other and their family. They selflessly gave of themselves and their resources, always being sacrificial givers.

Their personalities complemented each other. Both had a great sense of humor and hearty laughter. One had a gentle and kind heart, easily fooled at times (father). The other had a kind heart but was wise in recognizing troublemakers and was nobody's fool (mother).

One parent was deeply spiritual, leading a virtuous life founded on Christian teachings, though they never held a position in the Church or preached Christianity verbally. Through acts of generosity and unselfish giving, their actions spoke volumes (father). The other parent was deeply spiritual as well, actively involved in the Church, singing in the choir until late in life, holding leadership roles in Church organizations, and supporting and caring for those in need within the Church and the community. They judiciously distributed the resources provided by the kind generosity of the other parent. They sang, prayed, and bore witness to their faith every chance they got until the very end (mother).

Both parents loved deeply and fiercely. One parent was tender and intensely sentimental, remembering and chuckling over funny anecdotes, tearing up over warmth and sweet little nothings, and crying at partings (father). The other parent loved deeply and fiercely, with a love that was stern and practical, accepting the realities of the price of love—the pain of partings, the hurts, and the inherent disappointments in all human systems—families, friends, and social systems. They held their head up high, smiling on the outside while crying on the inside, stoically and with unwavering faith in God, never turning their back on those who relied on them or becoming cynical (mother).

When it comes to work ethics, both parents believed in doing their best, only the best, in everything they did, regardless of the circumstances, whether big or small.

So who am I like? Some days I feel more like my father, and other days I feel more like my mother. May my children and grandchildren see for themselves and draw their own conclusions.

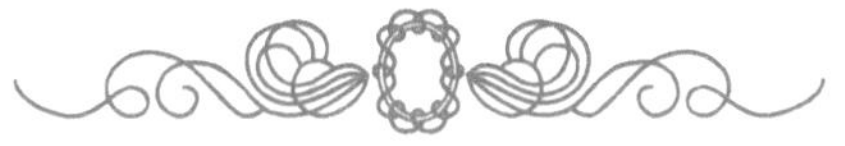

Remembering My Father

My dad is my hero, my role model, and the gold standard for a true gentleman. He is the most genuine, caring, hardworking, kind, generous, unselfish, and sensitive man I have ever known. With his great sense of humor, he could light up a room with his hearty laughter.

During my early childhood to late teenage years, my dad worked and lived abroad, only coming home every two years for a long three-month vacation. Our mother, who was the cornerstone and anchor of our family, held us together. Their marriage was incredible, built on love, care, mutual respect, and admiration for each other. Despite the physical distance, they remained close through the lengthy letters they wrote to each other, which they did many times during each month. Our mother generously shared stories from his letters, keeping him present in our daily lives. As soon as we learned to write letters, we began writing to him regularly.

Even though he was far away, we felt a sense of closeness through our letters, exchanging correspondence at least once a week. From the moment I started learning English, he insisted that I write to him in English. Initially, my letters were filled with broken English, poor grammar, and spelling mistakes. However, he would respond with equally loving letters in perfect English and beautiful handwriting. He kindly and gently corrected my errors without laughing or hurting my feelings. For instance, when I wrote to him about having a "style in my left eye," he responded, "I am so sorry that you have a stye in your left eye. I hope you've had the school nurse check on it by now."

Then he wrote that he was happy I was studying well and especially was taking an interest in learning English (English was only second language in my school in the '60s).

As a parting thought, he mentioned that he liked my style of writing and wished for me to always be in style. So I learned two additional meanings of the word *style* and also the correct spelling of *stye*. These were lessons taught with dignity and respect.

That was the nature of our relationship throughout the years. I cannot recall a single instance where we exchanged cross words. During the three-month vacations when he came home, he took us on family trips and allowed us to enjoy numerous fun and educational experiences in the state, such as visiting wildlife sanctuaries, museums, zoos, beaches, and more.

He taught me to treat success and failure with equal respect. In the face of failure, not to feel defeated but to accept it humbly, learning from it to conquer the next time. And in times of success, not to become too proud to the point of vanity.

I observed him living his life, and I learned. When he passed away at the age of eighty-one, I was only forty-nine, and the news of his passing shattered my world. Thanks to my precious daughter, I did not have to make that long flight home alone for his funeral. We had each other's shoulders to cry on throughout the journey from North Carolina to India.

I miss his love, compassion, sense of humor, wise advice, wisdom, and intense faith and love for his family. I am grateful to God for the true gift of a father that I am blessed to call (Entey Papa) *my papa*. I always referred to him as *my* papa as if he belonged to me and me alone. I miss how proud he was of me, how he cheered me on, and how he always had faith in me.

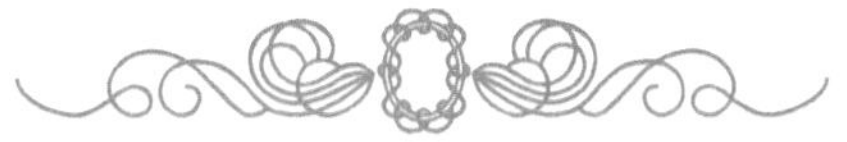

Remembering My Mother

My mother was the glue that held our family together. As the oldest of nine children, she was born and raised in a Christian family and married at a very young age, right after finishing high school. She entered into a family much smaller than the one she was accustomed to. My father, on the other hand, was one of four siblings, the youngest of three brothers and a younger sister. He worked overseas in a hospital run by an American company in Saudi Arabia. They got married during his vacation, and he returned after a three-month period. However, she had to stay behind as there were no accommodations for employees' families yet.

And so began her life as a wife, daughter-in-law, and sister-in-law, living in the family home with my father's parents. Her experiences at Nicholson High School, an all-girls' Christian boarding school, during her final year of high school, as well as her role as the oldest sibling to several younger siblings, prepared her to become the cornerstone of our family.

A few months later, my father was able to secure living arrangements for both of them through some miracle that allowed families to reside together. Despite being pregnant and alone, my young mother embarked on the long ship journey from India to Saudi Arabia. After the birth of my brother in 1946, I followed just fifteen months later in 1947. From my father's loving and admiring accounts, we learned that she managed the responsibilities of being a loving and attentive wife and mother with expertise.

They returned to India for my father's next three-month vacation, two years later. However, after the baptisms of both my brother and me and spending time with their parents, siblings, and my mother's family, my father had to return to his job in Saudi Arabia. Sadly and reluctantly, they accepted the fact that he had to leave in order to provide us with a good life.

They carried on with their married life for the next seventeen years, relying on weekly letters to stay in touch. As curious children, my sister and I would sneak peeks at the sweet letters our mother wrote, addressing them to "My darling" and signing off with "with all my love and prayers."

There was a two-year period when my sister was around two years old, and my mother and sister joined my father overseas. During those seventeen years, my brother and I spent those two years with our maternal grandparents, which was an amazing experience. Although we were away from our parents and paternal grandparents we knew, at around six and seven years of age, we found ourselves living in a different town and attending a new school. Instead of feeling scared or sad, we had the experience of a lifetime. We had loving grandparents, younger siblings of our mother who were closer in age to us and became like older siblings, and older ones who were married and closer in age to our parents.

When my mother and sister returned two years later, she was pregnant with our youngest brother. My father continued with his job for ten more years after our brother's birth. Selflessly, he did so to give us the best of everything, staying close through the wonderful letters he wrote and the long vacations home where he treated us to many of life's luxuries, such as vacations, fancy hotel stays, and dining at high-class restaurants.

My mother held our family together with courage, poise, and grace. She juggled so many roles, from being an attentive daughter-in-law to her grandparents, a loving sister-in-law to her uncles and aunts, a caring aunt to her cousins, and a loving yet firm disciplinarian to us, her four children.

She also maintained strong ties with her own birth family and would entertain various members in our home, allowing us to spend ample time with our maternal side of the family.

Fondly known as *Mother* (or *Mommy* to us, her children) by many young people in our small island community, she treated them lovingly and kindly, just as a mother would.

She managed her house, finances, and resources so well that I remember people coming to her to borrow money or household items when they were in need. Even at an early age, I noticed that she was nobody's fool. She was straightforward, setting limits and expectations in a tactful yet firm manner. People knew this about her, and there was always mutual respect.

She was deeply spiritual, and her faith was truly inspiring. Rather than preaching her faith, she lived it. In times of joy and challenging moments—of which she had plenty—she would transform into an incredible being. She remained humble in the face of good fortune and stood firm as a rock during trials, turning inward to her faith. Singing, praying, and facing challenges head-on, she exhibited unwavering strength.

With a great sense of humor, she laughed heartily and found joy in both small and big things in life. She knew how to make lemonade out of lemons when life presented her with challenges. I remember when the river flooded, and the water rose high enough to reach the road in front of our house, she was the first one to jump into the water and swim.

She deeply cared for people and always offered help to those in need. Even on her last day at the age of ninety-three, before passing away, she would call and check on her friends, neighbors, church members, and family.

She possessed remarkable leadership skills and actively participated in the women's group at church. She sang in the church choir for many years and was a highly respected and beloved member of our church and the community at large. I was in awe when I saw the multitude of people who attended her funeral—Christians, Hindus, people from all political parties, the rich and the poor, the young and the old, men and women.

She lives on in my heart alongside my amazing father. The examples they set through their lives surpass any lessons I could have learned from books. I consider myself truly blessed to have been born as their daughter.

If I could become even half the person my mother and father were, I would consider myself a decent human being.

Graceful Receivers

It was the 1970s when we still relied on paper charts and handwritten notes. I quickly discovered that those Paper Mate pens, which looked like pencils, did a great job. And they were affordable too! A pack of ten would only cost around $1.

I always kept them close by, whether it was in the pockets of my lab coat, on my desk at work, or a couple in my "hand bag" (that's what I called it back then, still adjusting to the American lingo—pocketbook, pen torch for flashlight, riding the lift for elevator to the twelfth-floor office, and so on).

During our first trip back to visit family in India, while we were out with my parents, my father needed a pen to write something. I reached into my bag and gave him one of my trusty Paper Mate pens. He loved the way it wrote. With his beautiful handwriting, I treasured the letters he wrote to me, filled with wisdom and good advice.

I tucked that little anecdote in my heart. When our next visit came a few years later, as I contemplated what gifts to bring home for the family, I thought, "Yes! A pack of Paper Mate pens!" It may have been inexpensive, but it was a thoughtful gesture considering how much he had appreciated the pen before.

And I was right! He loved it! The man who provided us with the best of everything cherished the gift of a pack of cheap Paper Mate pens from his daughter. You would have thought I had given him a Montblanc pen…ironic yet priceless. It was a lesson he taught me with his hearty huge smile.

He lived, and I learned. And I learned not just from his words, but more importantly, from his actions. This time, it was about being a "Graceful Receiver."

I am thankful for you, Papa. Thank God that I am blessed to be your daughter.

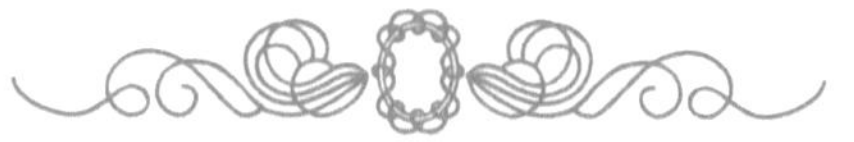

Friendships

And I am thankful to see how both of my children have picked amazing friends whom they love and care about and who love them and care about them too.

TRUE FRIENDS
ARE NEVER APART
MAYBE IN DISTANCE

———

Kumari Verghese

She hugged me, kissed me on my cheek, stepped back, and examined me from head to toe. A smile spread across her face as she expressed her happiness at our unexpected reunion after all these years.

I returned her hug and we stood there, reminiscing about those innocent days. We shared everything we could remember about our little classmates, teachers, and cute anecdotes.

On our way back home, my little five-year-old asked again, "But why was she so happy and excited to see you? Were you somebody important or something?"

I replied, "Yes, I was her friend. We sat on the same bench, learned the alphabet together, learned to read, write, and add numbers. We played tag together in the playground. That's what friendship is like—it makes you feel like somebody."

"Somebody important or something," she wondered.

I am truly blessed to have friends like that, from all walks of life.

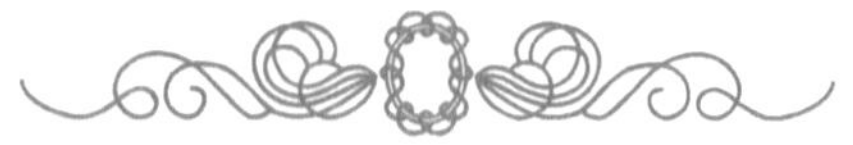

An Epic Class Reunion: KMC Pre-Med Class of '65, '66, and '67

Several years ago, in December 2015 to be exact, the pre-med class of 1965 held our fifty-year reunion along with two other classes—1966 and 1967. What unfolded was a truly magical three-day event at the Marriott in Bangalore, India. Friends reunited, many for the first time in thirty or forty years since leaving college. It was a stark contrast from the time we were single young adults with full heads of black hair, fit and trim, to now being older men and women with grey hair (or no hair in the case of many), appearing quite different, married, parents, and even grandparents, with some sadly widowed.

But deep within our hearts, we were transported back to the late teens and young adults who first met on the college campus fifty years ago. After exchanging warm hugs and shedding tears of joy, we indulged in reminiscing while gathering for coffee, formal meals, introductions, entertainment, music, and dancing. We made sure to capture these moments in photographs, seeking to preserve the memories of this special occasion.

There was also a competition to contribute to the fifty-year souvenir, and I was fortunate enough to win with an article I titled "The Amazing Tapestry." As a result, I received this iPad Mini, which has become a vessel for countless stories I have written over the past several years.

With hearts full of love, gratitude, admiration, and excitement, we shared our life stories in person. The memories of this once-in-a-lifetime experience have woven new colors and threads into the fabric of this beautiful tapestry called friendship. And this incredible tapestry will continue to bring joy to our hearts until we meet again.

Dr. Kumari Verghese ('65 Batch)

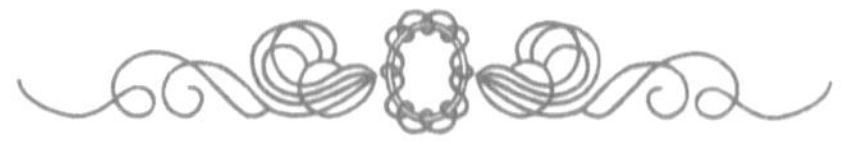

Fifty-Year Reunion Souvenir: Anecdotes and Tributes

Anecdotes and Tributes for Reunion Souvenir

1. Krishnankutty and His Taxi Cab

It was a few weeks into their Manipal life when seven Malayalee classmates, who had become quite close by then, heard that a Malayalam movie was playing in a theater in Udupi. They decided to catch a taxi and all seven of them piled into it, fitting in two layers. Communicating with the driver in broken Kannada, they suddenly heard one wise individual among the group say in Malayalam, "Oh my God! What are we doing? How do we know we can trust this guy? For all we know, he may take us somewhere and who knows what he might do?!" This statement was met with a collective gasp from the rest of the group, as they too began to speculate about the possible risks involved. None of them noticed the emerging smile on the driver's face until he could no longer contain it.

The driver finally spoke, saying, "Young ladies, my name is Krishnan Kutty. I am a Malayalee too! I would never harm you. You can count on me to get you there safely and bring you back safely. You can call me anytime you need a taxi. Remember, even if you go to the moon, you will find a Malayalee there, be it a taxi driver or a tea shop owner or anything else!"

This revelation sparked laughter that turned into tears of joy for the rest of the journey to Udupi. They enjoyed the movie and had dinner at Komals afterward. True to his words, Krishnan Kutty safely returned them to Saroj Sadan.

And so began their agreement with their personal taxi driver.

2. Raman the Engineering College Boy and His Friends, Enemies of the Cobra

A group of hostel mates and friends, returning to their rooms from the mess hall after dinner, suddenly came to a halt upon hearing a shrill scream from one of the girls who was ahead. She had entered her room only to find a cobra coiled up with its head held high. Naturally, the rest of the group reacted with equally loud screams, emanating from the throats of these seemingly delicate young girls. Soon enough, the staff, which included a watchman, cook, and servers, came running to see what was happening.

A few engineering students who, for unknown reasons, enjoyed taking post-dinner walks near Saroj Sadan also heard the commotion. One student, who preferred to be called Raman, grabbed a stick and scaled the wall, with a few others following suit. Meanwhile, one of the servers known as Akkas ran and fetched a coconut shell with rice, red chili, and other items for a ritual offering. Raman and his team fearlessly dealt with the unwelcome visitor while Akka exclaimed some things in Tulu or Kannada that the girls who understood the language deemed less than complimentary toward Raman and his team. However, in the eyes of the girls, they were doing just fine.

3. The Case of the Misplaced Sarees

Not long after the Cobra incident, late into the night, the girls at Saroj Sadan were engrossed in their homework. Suddenly, they heard noise outside on the street—a group of men singing an off-key Malayalam Christian funeral song, "Samayamam Radhathil Njan." Curiosity prompted them to look out the window, where they witnessed a group of men carrying a person in a recumbent position, undoubtedly the deceased (may his soul rest in peace). Their hearts went out to the deceased and his family and friends, until they overheard one of the carriers exclaim, "Eda entae chappals poy" (translation: "Hey, buddy, your slippers are gone!"). This remark was followed by uproarious laughter as the carriers dropped the slipper-less corpse and dispersed in different directions.

Days later, a few girls were unwinding by the serene Manipal lake after a long, hard week of school. They noticed some clumsily-dressed young women parading by. Something seemed off—were they not wearing the sarees properly? Did they not walk like real women? Were they even women? Then it hit them—weren't those the same sarees that had mysteriously vanished from some of their first-floor rooms? One by one, the women undressed, revealing that they had cleverly worn the sarees over their pants and shirts. Clumsily, they folded the sarees and handed them over to the girls.

It turned out that these women had managed to acquire the sarees through an open window, using sticks and coat hangers during the earlier funeral fiasco.

And that's how the bookshelves ended up closer to the window, while the clothes shelves and hangers were moved toward the inner wall side.

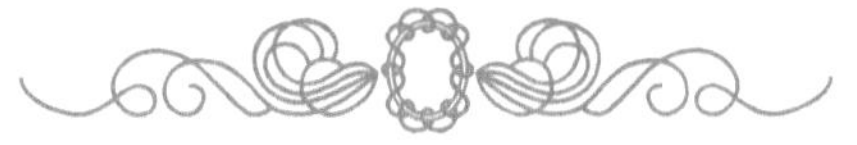

My First Big Trip

I obtained my very first passport in 1972, at the age of twenty-five. Fresh out of medical school, I married a man whom I had met for possibly an hour, in my parents' home as per prior arrangement between both our families. Although we both had the choice to say yes or no, we agreed that we were ready to say yes. Ten days later, we were married.

We were total strangers. He lived in Chicago, Illinois, USA, and I lived in Kerala, India. He had to return to the USA in two months, and I had to complete my internship in Kerala within the next ten months. I had never wanted or fancied going abroad, or even leaving the state. For whatever reasons, we chose to marry each other. At the end of his two-month vacation, he left for the USA, and I returned to my internship at the nearest medical college from home.

The two months we spent together were a whirlwind. Honeymoon at the famous Kovalam beach, a lot of traveling within the state and out of state, visiting families. We got to know each other to some degree and even enjoyed each other's company. By the end of those two months, we had become quite fond of each other and started to feel sad that we would soon have to part ways for a very long time, until I could complete my internship, obtain my passport, and visa to travel abroad.

So we tearfully parted ways, agreeing to keep in touch regularly via airmail letters that took a week or more to reach our respective destinations. The year was 1972, and international phone calls were not easily accessible.

As we returned to our separate lives and kept our promises of weekly letters, we strangely felt closer to each other despite the distance. We missed each other, wanted to be together, and began counting the days.

The preparations began at both ends. He had to start the paperwork to sponsor me, his wife, for an immigration visa to the USA, and I had to apply for a passport to travel abroad. Several weeks went by, and finally, my passport arrived. I still had to wait for the visa while also completing my internship.

Once I received the call from the US consulate in Madras, I traveled to Madras with my beloved father for the visa interview. It was during this interview that another reality struck me hard in the heart, nearly punching a hole.

My beloved family, my home, my beautiful island village, my extended family, my friends—all of these precious people and places are not getting a visa to the USA. I will leave all of these behind and go to a faraway land to make a home for myself with my husband. I was crushed.

Then his mother, widowed five years prior and planning to travel with us to join five of her six children in the USA, reminded me that my husband, the youngest of six and the only son, planned to return to Kerala after a few years, and we would live in their home just a few miles from my parents and the home I loved so much. That was music to my ears.

Once my internship was over and both our visas arrived, at the end of eleven long months and hundreds of love letters on blue aerograms, we started planning our journey.

I would say goodbye to my parents and siblings and go to my mother-in-law's home to get ready to leave together.

My parents would come to her house the night before to take the early morning ride to the airport. My older brother, his wife, and their nine-month-old twin sons, as well as my younger brother, would also travel with us to the airport. My sister and her family lived out of state in New Delhi and would meet us at the Delhi airport during our layover.

That last night together with my parents at my mother-in-law's house was the beginning of a heartache that I will carry for the rest of my life. As the three of us slept together in the guest room, we talked and talked, choking up and laughing alternately. My mother would hug me so tight each time Cleo, our dog, howled, knowing that he was to leave home the next morning to stay at a family friend's home since my mother was packing up and leaving.

My father would choke up and say, "He is heartbroken too, just like us."

At the airport, we hugged each other—all six of us adults and the little nine-month-olds too. They waved and said, "Mommy Tata" as my mother-in-law and I walked toward the plane to board. They called their mother "Amma" and I was "Mommy" before I even became Mommy.

As the plane took off, I felt a huge lump in my throat. Looking through the small window, through teary eyes, I saw the family I loved like I had never loved anyone else vanish into small specks amidst hundreds of specks.

That longing to see them and hug them one more time would become a reality that I would live with during happy times and sad times in the new land I eventually called home and raise my own family in.

At the other end of the nearly 36-hour journey across oceans and long layovers, awaited the man I married. A son reuniting with his mother, a husband reuniting with his wife.

Tucked away in the treasure chest of my heart would be the pain of separation from a love like no other—my family—a treasure that I would always cherish as I began a new love and a new life.

Where my first big journey began and ended, many travels alone and with family would follow—by plane with passports and visas and pricey air tickets.

There is also a place I can travel to and from anytime I want to, no air tickets, passport, or visa required. Whether with closed eyes or while watching a sunrise or sunset, a beautiful full moon, a rainbow, or floating clouds over blue skies—a glance through the rearview mirror of my heart—my sweet home, the wonderful family, and the beautiful island village I left behind.

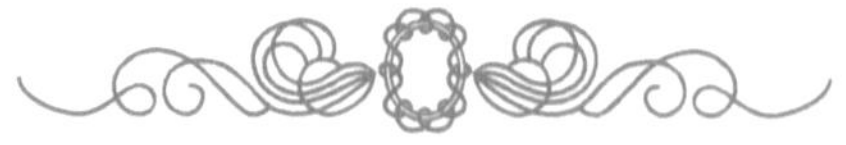

My First Job Interview
The Stepping-Stone to
an Amazing Practice
Experience in NC

Friends have always played a significant role in my life. They have been a true blessing in every sense of the word. As I was nearing the end of my child psychiatry fellowship in Michigan, my husband and I decided to relocate our family of four to a warmer place once I completed my training.

With Dr. Tanas, Clinical Director, John Umstead Hospital, Butner,
NC (my first boss July 1980) and colleagues from 1980 to 2020.
Associate Director, Dementia Unit, Gero Psychiatry, JUH, Butner, NC
With Dr. Tanas at my retirement tea

We mentioned our plans to Sasi, a friend who used to live in Chicago but had moved to North Carolina. He shared how happy his family was with their move and suggested that we consider North Carolina as a place to call home. Additionally, Lizzy, another psychiatrist and friend living in Delaware, suggested I get in touch with her friend, Dr. Sounder, a psychiatrist who had recently moved to North Carolina upon hearing about our job search plans in the state. She provided me with his contact number in North Carolina.

My husband, a research scientist, and I, a fellow in psychiatry set to graduate in June '80, took the opportunity to update our curriculum vitae, gathered a couple of reference letters each, and reached out to Dr. Sounder. He was aware of openings for adult psychiatrists at the hospital where he worked but was uncertain about any positions for child psychiatrists. However, he shared the contact information for the clinical director, Dr. Tanas. I promptly called Dr. Tanas and had a pleasant conversation with him. He suggested I complete the application and come in for a formal interview. Although there was no immediate opening for a child psychiatrist, he proposed starting in the adult division with the possibility of transitioning to the child division when a position became available.

Taking an extra workday off along with the Memorial Day weekend in May '80, just before my graduation in June, we flew to North Carolina with our preschool-aged son and infant daughter. Our kind friends Sasi and Uma graciously hosted us at their home. While Sasi's mother looked after our children, I accompanied Sasi for an interview with Dr. Tanas at John Umstead Hospital in Butner, North Carolina, a town adjacent to Sasi's workplace in Creedmoor, North Carolina. (Meanwhile, my husband had his own interview at Duke University Hospital in Durham, North Carolina.)

Dr. Tanas thoroughly reviewed my CV and the reference letters, conducted an interview, and asked if I could return after lunch to meet with the credentials committee. Coincidentally, he mentioned that it was the committee's monthly meeting and wanted a few others to meet me as well.

Although I was nervous about meeting with the entire committee, I knew I had to wait until Sasi finished his work to pick me up at the end of the day. Therefore, I agreed to the arrangement. Dr. Tanas kindly arranged for me to go first in front of the committee before they proceeded with their usual agenda. I don't remember who asked what, but each of those physician members had a question or two, or more. I also noticed that they passed around the reference letters and my CV, which each of them reviewed quite intensely. Contrary to my rapid heartbeat and nervous answers at the outset, it turned out to be a pleasant exchange by the end of an hour that I later learned to be the beginning of my forty-year career in public sector psychiatry.

As I waited for Sasi to pick me up, I wondered what they were saying behind closed doors. Would I get the job, or would I need to explore other options in North Carolina since we were certain North Carolina was the place we wanted to call home? Dr. Tanas had mentioned that he would inform me of the committee's decision via letter.

Thankfully, their committee meeting concluded before my ride arrived. Dr. Tanas spotted me waiting in the waiting room on his way out. My heart raced as he kindly walked over and said, "Dr. Verghese, you come highly recommended. I was pleased with your interview, and our committee unanimously recommended that I offer you the job!" I was immensely grateful and knew in my heart that it was the pure grace and the will of God that placed me there in that time and place.

For the next forty years, I would serve the state's most troubled and underserved mentally ill population in a variety of settings. It began with that first job in the adult admission unit of one of the state's four psychiatric hospitals. Then I moved on to the geriatric psychiatric unit, followed by co-directorship of the dementia unit. After a brief but fulfilling stint with Nash General Psychiatry Department, I returned to the public sector as an attending psychiatrist at Dorothea Dix Hospital. Later, I became the chief of service for their geriatric psychiatry division, and finally transitioned to community psychiatry in Smithfield, North Carolina, where I served in various capacities, including medical director of the mental health center, inpatient director for the hospital's behavioral health unit, and consultant to hospital units and the emergency room. I retired in 2015, but retirement lasted only two months as I returned to work for Johnston County Health Department, providing outpatient services and consultation services to the hospital emergency room.

Wrapping up the last year of my forty-year public service was a year that I will always remember in awe. From 2019 to 2020, I worked as a consultant psychiatrist for the North Carolina Department of Public Safety, Prison Systems. It was the most humbling, gratifying, and almost spiritual experience in all of my practice. Seeing the prisoners, hearing their stories, and feeling in my heart how each of us are children of God, and that it is His grace that sustains us, made me feel incredibly humble, non-judgmental, and grateful. My heart went out to each of those individuals. I wished them well, prayed for them to find peace and healing, and prayed for God to guide them in choosing the right medications. They expressed feeling better, and I felt good knowing that I was making a difference.

Then the pandemic hit our nation. Knowing that I was in the so-called "vulnerable and high-risk age group," being seventy-three years old, sadly, with a heavy heart and cracking voice, I said goodbye to them. I also said goodbye to my first boss, Dr. Tanas, who, after retirement, was working as a consultant and my peer at the Department of Public Safety, Prison Systems. Ironically, my last boss at Dorothea Dix Hospital, Dr. Sheitman, was also our boss at DPS! (I didn't have another boss since leaving Dorothea Dix Hospital as I was the boss from then until retiring in 2015.) It felt like I had come full circle. As sad as it was to leave a career that I loved so much, I was also glad that it ended the way it did.

Medical Director, Behavioral Health Division, Johnston Co Health Dept, Smithfield, North Carolina. At retirement tea, February 2015.

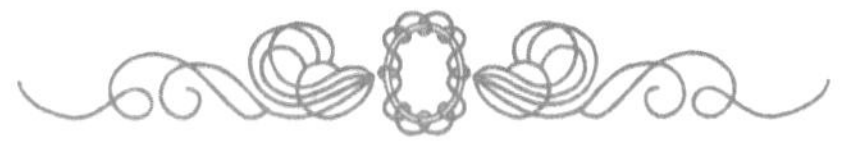

My First Boss

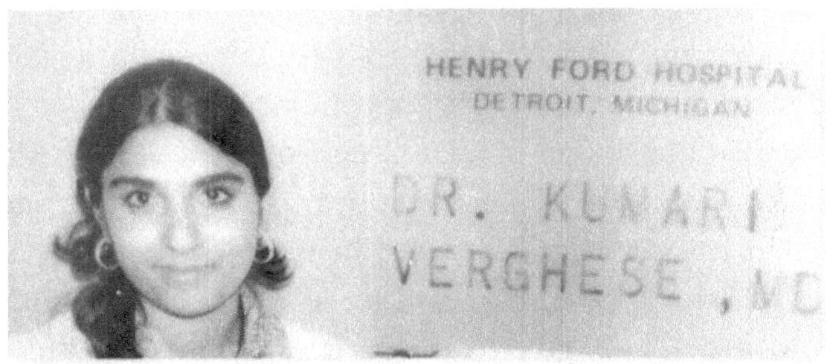

From residency to retirement, 1975–2020—a span of forty-five years: five years dedicated to residency and fellowship at two hospitals in Michigan, followed by forty years serving as an attending in various roles at four hospitals and three clinics in North Carolina. What an incredible blessing it has been to have such a rich and fulfilling experience, working alongside attendings, directors, and colleagues throughout my career.

I found your version of this sentiment in my very first boss, Dr. John J. A Vietnam veteran, husband, father, and a specialized psychiatrist—an amazing attending to a very nervous and timid twenty-seven-year-old first-year resident in psychiatry.

Everything I learned about the practice of psychiatry, I learned from Dr. J.

It was July 1975 at Henry Ford Hospital in Detroit, Michigan. I was assigned to cover the July Fourth holiday weekend in the inpatient psychiatric services, which consisted of thirty-two beds, two attendings, and two residents. Straight out of two days of orientation on July 1 and 2, I was the one scheduled to see all the patients on the unit and respond to calls from other floors and the ER regarding patients with psychiatric issues.

I was petrified! My face must have revealed my fear and apprehension, and Dr. J sensed it. He kindly and reassuringly told me that he would be my backup and that there was nothing he would consider an "unnecessary call" if I needed his advice.

To my surprise, and thanks to silent prayers and Dr. J's confidence in me, the weekend was uneventful. His kindness, confidence, and respect towards me, a junior doctor whom he had only met three days prior, gave me the confidence to carry out my duties with kindness and respect towards my patients and peers.

I watched him interview our patients, interact with team members, and communicate with fellow physicians from other specialties. One particular early event is etched in my memory. We responded promptly to an ER consult regarding a very violent patient. Dr. J calmly and respectfully greeted the patient by his last name, addressing him as Mr. (his name). The patient, with both fists clenched, pounded Dr. J in the chest, saying, "I don't need you."

Dr. J took a couple of steps back, composed himself, and responded calmly. "You scared me there, but I'm okay now, and I'll be here when you're ready to talk with me. You seem upset, and it might help if you share your concern with me. I won't hurt you."

Something touched a chord in that patient's heart. He took a deep breath, got back on the bed, and gestured for Dr. J to come closer so "we can talk." He also allowed me, the sidekick, to move closer so I could hear his story.

When the interview was over, the ER doctor noticed that Dr. J's shirt was torn from the patient pulling on it as he walked away from the punch.

They took an x-ray of his chest before we returned to our unit, with Dr. J wearing a hospital gown in place of a shirt. We continued rounds. In the meantime, his shirt was washed, dried, and mended by one of the nurses on our unit. Thankfully, the x-ray came back okay.

In one morning, I witnessed the incredible humanity of a respected senior physician being attacked by a very disturbed person who himself was frightened. Dr. J admitting that he too was scared and assuring the patient that he would not retaliate made the patient feel comfortable enough to let his guard down.

I saw caregivers caring for caregivers, team members coming together for one another. Compassion prevailed over aggression and anger.

Humility triumphed over vanity—hospital gown over dress shirt and tie. Grace and professionalism endured under intense pressure.

I will always remember Dr. J's kindness, bedside manners, depth of knowledge, teamwork spirit, respect, confidence, clinical skills, eagerness to teach, and so many more incredible attributes.

This laid the foundation upon which I built my own practice, adding my personal touches as I progressed through the various roles I was blessed to be in as a psychiatrist.

As a retiree with forty-five years of service to people suffering from a wide spectrum of mental and behavioral health issues, I feel blessed to look back and remember the amazing Dr. John, as well as every boss I learned so much from thereafter.

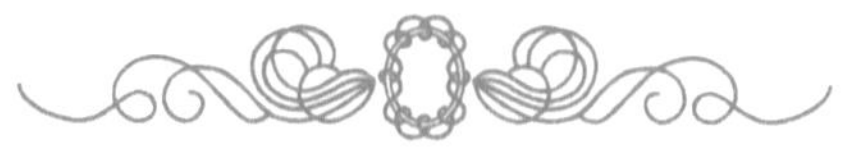

My First Live Concert and the Ones That Followed

I've had the opportunity to witness a few of my favorite musicians perform live. I thoroughly enjoyed each one, starting with the Carpenters in 1978 in Michigan, followed by Andy Gibb, Roy Orbison, Rod Stewart, Phil Collins, Paul Simon, Reba McEntire, and Bette Midler. Each concert was memorable for various reasons, whether it was the company I was with, the venue, a beloved song, a nostalgic memory brought to life, or a journey down memory lane.

The very first concert that our family of three attended, with my husband, myself, and our four-year-old son, stands out in my heart. We went with our dear friends Carl and Laura Lee to see siblings Richard and Karen Carpenter perform their clean and uplifting songs in the wide-open amphitheater on a beautiful summer evening in Michigan. It holds a special place in my heart because of the pure joy and excitement it brought to our innocent child, as well as the love and tender care our friends showed toward our son (Laura Lee later became his Sunday school teacher). Whenever I hear any of the Carpenters' best songs, like "On Top of the World," I will always think of these caring and considerate friends and the innocence and pure joy reflected in our little four-year-old's smile and laughter.

Then there was the Bette Midler concert we attended at Walnut Creek Amphitheater in Raleigh, North Carolina, with our friends Bob and Leslie. This was after her movie *Beaches* and her hit song "Wind Beneath My Wings." Our little daughter had sternly warned us, "I'll never forgive you if you see this movie without me." So the first chance we got to watch the movie together on an overseas flight to visit family in India, we did so, sharing laughter and tears.

Years later, as we watched Ms. Midler perform in Raleigh, I couldn't help but shed tears when she belted out "The Rose." It reminded me of that plane ride, the little girl who sat beside me, and the laughter and tears we shared. I had to turn on my little flip phone, dial her number, and let her listen in, so she wouldn't have to forgive me for hearing that favorite song without her.

Special too was my very first live concert in NC, featuring one of my favorite musicians, Rod Stewart. I attended the concert with my best friend Charlotte at Walnut Creek Amphitheater on a beautiful fall night. We sat on a quilt spread over the thick grass and enjoyed every one of Rod Stewart's hit songs. I was so captivated by the performance that I decided to lie down flat on my back to also appreciate the visual delights of the starlit Carolina sky. I remember telling Charlotte, "Wow! This must be the first time I'm seeing the night sky with a beautiful moon and uninterrupted stars since leaving home." As I missed my family and loved ones back in India, Rod Stewart started playing his next song, and my heart was overwhelmed with a tsunami of emotions as he performed "May the Good Lord Be with You," as if to echo my sentiments.

That song has always been a favorite of mine, my go-to song for my precious children, and now my grandchildren as well. I could hardly contain myself when my daughter and son-in-law chose to honor me with this song as they introduced "the parents of the bride" at their wedding.

Songs and hymns will always be ingrained in my soul. They keep the people dear to me close to my heart, as close as the next breath. I am incredibly grateful for the artists, writers, composers, and the beautiful people I have been blessed to share these musical journeys with.

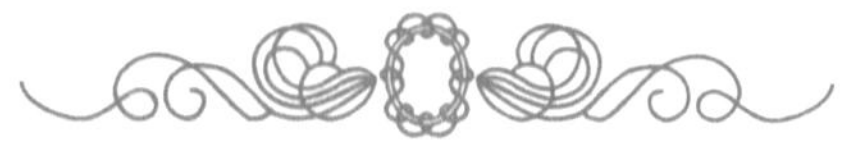

Memories of Our Epic Reunion: A Walk in the Garden

A Walk in the Garden

In the midst of a vast field, unbounded by fences or high walls, stood an incredible garden—an oasis of flowers in a glorious array of colors and fragrances. Planted by the master gardener over half a century ago, these beautiful plants have grown to bear flowers and fruits for all those in need to enjoy. Some have fulfilled their purpose sooner, having completed their mission in the field. They may have faced more thorns, but their roses outshone the challenges.

For a brief span of three days, a gentle breeze called the friends for life to take a walk in this garden. It was an unforgettable experience—to touch, to feel, to walk beside each other, and to share the stories of lives well lived and battles fought. Time stood still in the face of such a formidable bond.

As their eyes met, many filled with tears of joy, and their arms held each other in warm embraces, half a century vanished into thin air. Their hearts leaped with pure joy, and their souls feasted on the stories they shared. Even unspoken words and their mere togetherness spoke volumes. Then they parted ways, with hearts full of joy, carrying the ache of parting and a yearning for more. Having walked in that garden, their lives will never be the same. They savor the memories of rekindled friendships, and their hearts care deeper for and wish well-being upon their cherished friends.

Until the next walk in that garden, may the gentle breeze carry their stories and the showers of connectedness keep their garden alive and blooming.

Dedicated to the KMC class of '65, '66, and '67: I am forever blessed for having had you in my life.

Kumari Verghese, MD
Class of '65

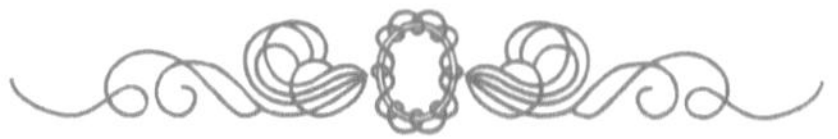

An Amazing Tapestry— Med-School Days

This is the one for which I won the iPad Mini—an unexpected honor as the top pick for our fifty-year reunion souvenir of the pre-med class of '65, '66, and '67. I was genuinely shocked! Perhaps there weren't many options to choose from?

An Amazing Tapestry

As teens, they gathered as strangers in a small campus town, far away from the comforts of home, family, and friends. Young, naive, and somewhat shy, they dared to weave a beautiful tapestry—one that was vibrant and inviting, soft and delicate, yet resilient enough to withstand the tests of time and distance. It became a source of visual delight and emotional warmth.

United by their differences and shared interests, this intricate fabric of friendship endured through a life filled with new beginnings, adventures, ups and downs. From schoolwork to successes, failures, the joys of first love, and the pain of lost love, they experienced it all together. They learned, laughed, cried, and even prayed side by side, transcending the limits imposed by religion or creed.

But the time came for them to part ways at the end of their school years. With bittersweet tears, they bid farewell, vowing never to let life's events or physical distance sever the threads of that beautiful tapestry they called "friends for life." They knew in their hearts that this amazing creation would envelop them in love, whether in each other's presence or out of sight.

Their love spanned across cities, towns, and continents. They shared their lives, defying the barriers of time and space. Their hearts ached for the few who were called to their eternal homes prematurely, cherishing their memory through fond recollections.

Now, half a century later, they gather once again—not as young, nervous strangers, but as accomplished professionals with silvered hair, as parents and grandparents. Their hearts brim with love, gratitude, admiration, and excitement as they prepare to share their life stories in person. The memories of this once-in-a-lifetime experience will interweave new colors and threads into the fabric of this beautiful tapestry. And the amazing tapestry called "friends for life" will keep their hearts brimming with joy until they meet again.

Dr. Kumari Verghese ('65 Batch)

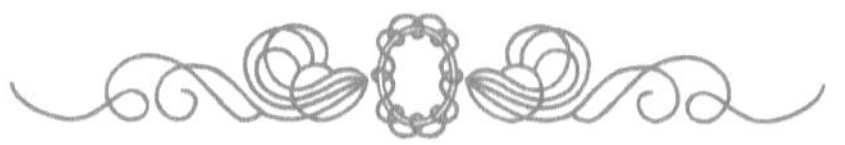

The Church of My Choice

Why St. Paul's? Why support the capital campaign?

Being raised in a Christian family in Kerala, India, prayer was always an integral part of my life. Family prayers at dawn and dusk followed a pattern in our multigenerational household. The elders sat on chairs while the children rolled a mat on the floor and sat down after completing their duties—collecting and distributing the Bible, hymn books, and the prayer book to all the appropriate people. Then we followed the routine: singing one or two hymns, reading from the Old or New Testament, and reciting a psalm. Either my father or mother would say or read the prayer, and the Lord's Prayer would be recited by all. Finally, my grandfather would conclude with a dismissal.

Sunday school for children and attending church as a family were a given on Sundays. There was only one service, which was rather long. Everyone sat through the announcements and brief meetings at times after the service. We had a chance to witness how the church was made up of the people, and how the people took care of each other—not just the church members, but also anyone in our community who had special needs. They helped send kids to school, sponsored meals for the bystanders in an entire ward of the nearby general hospital, and assisted in sending needy individuals for special medical or surgical care. They visited the sick at home and prayed with them. They attended baptisms, weddings, and funerals, and were a part of each other's lives in so many ways. They respected and took good care of the clergy, always ready to respond to calls for sharing their time, treasure, and talents.

When we moved to North Carolina from Michigan in the summer of 1980, with our almost six-year-old son and six-month-old daughter, we wanted to find a church home similar to the one we were accustomed to in Kerala. A church where the people were the church and took care of each other—an all-inclusive church. After visiting a few other churches, we joined St. Luke's Episcopal Church in Durham. We were blessed to have had both Bishop Bob Johnson and Bishop Anne Hodges Copple as our past priests during our time in Durham.

When we moved to Cary in '95, we didn't have to search for an Episcopal Church since our friends in Cary, Alex and Lilly Mathew, along with their three sons, were already members at St. Paul's, and we followed suit. We have been blessed to be part of this church ever since.

So why St. Paul's? Because it feels like the church "back home." The messages, ministries, mission, and the dedication and commitment of the clergy and parish—all contribute to this feeling. As a retired physician specializing in psychiatry, I see how spirituality is such an integral part of our mental health, and how many of my patients struggle with emotional pain and deep loneliness. It is not uncommon for them to respond with "just myself" when I ask who is there for them. I am incredibly grateful for our church and the incredible outreach ministries we undertake. I am also thankful for all the work within the church that nourishes people of all ages.

Why give? "For where your treasure is, there your heart will be also" (Matthew 6:21).

The campaign with its vision spoke to our hearts. So prayerfully we considered and happily pledged to support the vision according to our means from God's gifts that we have been blessed to be stewards of.

Chapel at Balikamatom Boarding School

St. Paul's Episcopal Church, Cary, North Carolina

My hometown church where many life events in our family
are celebrated and my parents and ancestors are buried

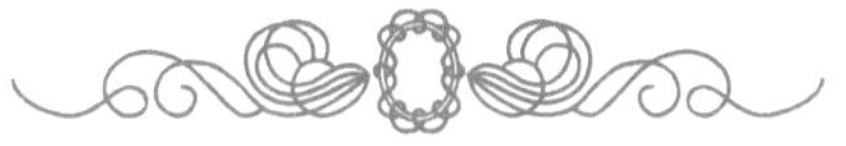

The Day My World Came Crashing Down

August 9, 1996, Friday. The start of a usual weekend. I had just come home to Apex from my out-of-town work in Rocky Mount for the weekend. Tisha was working at Macaroni Grill. Tikku was in college. So Babuji and I went out for dinner to a favorite Mexican restaurant.

It was a slow evening, and we took our time getting home. The red alert light on the land phone was blinking, letting us know that there was a message waiting. I picked up the phone and listened to the message: "This is Kochaniyan calling for Kumari Daniel (he sounded anxious and disorganized, even forgetting my married name)."

He said it was urgent that we call back a certain number since the phone at my parents' home was out of order. I called that number, which belonged to a neighbor. He rambled something about Appachen passing and gave the phone to my sweet little brother, Bakuttan, who, between sobs, told me that our precious Papa had passed away that morning.

My life turned upside down in that moment. No, not my papa. He can't go. No. Not now. Not ever.

A calm resolve came over me as I moved about the next few hours. Driven by one goal, the goal of going home to see him one last time, I had to get things in order. Patiently, calmly, and methodically, I put into motion a whole host of activities. I called my practice partner and informed him of the need for me to go home for two weeks. Dr. Cunningham was a kind Christian man who agreed wholeheartedly to cover my patients in my absence. I checked the passport and visa—the passport was okay, but the visa had expired. That meant a trip to Washington, DC, to get the visa. So a flight needed to be booked via Washington, DC.

I packed a carry-on bag for the trip. Then I called close friends who have been like family here—Sasi and Reema, Jose and Valsa, Alex and Lillykutty, Philip and Ramani, George and Bavakutty, Charlotte and John. They came one by one, as late as it was.

Tisha pulled up after work, walked in wondering why all the cars were there, and noticed that all our friends looked somber and sad. She walked upstairs to the master bedroom where I was finishing getting my handbag ready—wallet, passport, and other personal items. Seeing each other shattered all restraints. We hugged each other tightly and cried through broken hearts. As I informed her that I would be leaving to see Papa off on his final journey, that sixteen-year-old stoic heart informed me that she is coming too, miss school or not, she is coming.

We checked her passport. Our hearts sank as we noted that both her passport and visa had expired. It didn't matter to her, she was coming. We could go to DC and get both on the same day, except that it was almost 10:00 p.m. on Friday, and the next day, Saturday, they may not be open for service at the passport and visa (Indian consulate) offices. That didn't matter to her either—she was coming, we could try, they may open for emergencies. So she, too, packed a bag. Sasi volunteered to drive us to DC overnight, taking turns driving with Babuji. Anu came along to give us moral support.

We called our friends Jaffer and Sheela in Potomac, Maryland. They opened their home for us to stay whenever we reached there. Calls were made to the US passport office and Indian consular offices in the morning on Saturday. They agreed to meet us and issue the passport and visas. Air tickets were secured for evening flights to India.

It was pure divine intervention that we had angels on earth at every step to make that trip possible with such ease. It was amazing that Tisha, with her strong will and determination and her deep love for her grandparents and family, kept her optimism to guide our plans. Her love, kindness, and concern for us drove her to not let us take that trip alone.

At the other end of the trip, a day later, our beloved Bakuttan waited to pick us up from the airport. With broken hearts, we all went to see our precious Papa at the hospital's mobile mortuary. He looked so peaceful and serene, as if he was sleeping. As we left the hospital, leaving him there, the reality finally hit us. He is not coming home, except to come home tomorrow, carried in to lay in his bed in the drawing room, where we all sit around singing hymns, reading scriptures, and praying as people come in to pay respect to him. Then they will move him to the large pavilion in the front yard where more people will come, priests will pray, and he will be carried into the van for his final journey to the church. We will travel in the van with him. I looked at that face all the way to the church. His calm, peaceful face.

A scene from the time we spent in the drawing room, prior to moving him to the outside pavilion, is etched in my heart forever. It is a testament to my mother's faith, her courage, composure, and stoicism. It also speaks to our reliance on scriptures for all times, especially during times of grief and trials. It was fitting that I picked one of my favorite Psalms - Psalm 121. Though I could only get through half of verse one before I broke down.

The rest of the day and the days that followed were blurry. It was wonderful to be with family to grieve together, reminisce, and celebrate together. Then the day came for Tisha and me to return to the US. I am forever grateful that we had each other's shoulder to cry on as we made that two-day trip back to DC.

Waiting at the receiving end was the four-and-a-half-year-old who adored Papa and followed him around, seeing him as his hero during the six months of his stay with them in India. Now, at age twenty-two, in college, he missed coming to bid Papa goodbye due to his own struggles. As we walked into the arrival gate, his grief-stricken face met us, and all three of us cried bitter tears. The drive home to Cary was interrupted a few times as he pulled over to the side when a new wave of grief and guilt hit him.

Back safely at home, everybody returned to their lives, grieving in their own way. As for me, that grief and missing him have become just as much a part of me as I cherish the joy of the wonderful memories of my amazing father. It was a lesson in finding comfort in faith through scriptures.

So here I was, thinking that I was the favorite child (apparently the other three thought they were each the favorite too!). This is my chance to pay tribute to my precious father. I opened the Bible, turned to one of my favorite psalms, Psalm 121. I must have gotten to "I lift up my eyes to the hills" when a lump in my throat broke into a huge sob. Someone else took the Bible from me and read on the rest.

I felt a soft pat on my back and heard my mom's gentle, calm voice again, saying, "This would have broken Papa's heart. We cannot weep like those who have lost hope" (and the rest of the verse I don't remember).

Now sixteen years later at age eighty-eight, our mother of four, grandmother of eleven, and great-grandmother of sixteen prays constantly, thanks God for all the blessings she enjoys—the greatest of all she believes is "that good man" whose hand she held onto as she walked up the steps to the family home, how he cared for her, how she respects him, and how the wonderful life memories with him never let her feeling lonely or sad.

And now when I hear Psalm 121, I smile sometimes and think of another verse: "Ye of little faith" and feel a little embarrassed. Then along with my other favorite psalm, Psalm 23, I rejoice that we have the Book of Life to help us navigate our lives through any storms of life.

"Our Father in heaven, we thank you for all fathers, mothers, husbands, wives, children, grandchildren, families, friends and even the strangers among us. Help us to be a reflection of Your love as we go about playing the roles that You have blessed us with. In Your Son's name we pray. Amen!"

January 15, '12

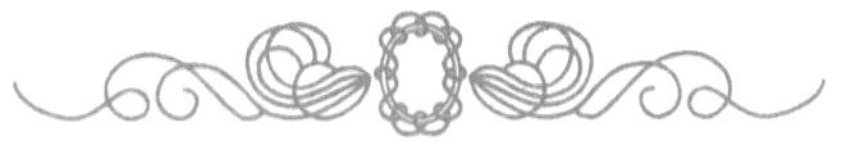

The Day My World Crashed
the Second Time

It was an ordinary morning. She woke up at dawn as usual. After morning routines, she sat on the cane chair by her bedside, placed a prayer cloth over her head, and prayed. If you were a fly on the wall, you would hear her softly thanking God for all the blessings she enjoys, even listing the many things that are often taken for granted. Then she asks for God's blessings on her family, friends, and the families of friends. She also prays for anyone she knows who has a special need or challenge.

Then she had a cup of coffee brought to her by her very attentive younger daughter, with whom she was living for close to two or three years. She then equipped her walker with the day's necessities—her medications, phone book, and phone—carefully placing them in a walker pocket/pouch lovingly made for her by her other daughter's dear friend, Charlotte.

She walked over cautiously to the living room and sat in her usual spot on the sofa. Her daughter and one of her grandsons, who had stopped by to check on her, joined her, and they talked about all things big and small. Then she had breakfast and returned to the living room. They talked again, reminiscing, laughing, and enjoying each other's company.

She wanted an early bath and asked her helper to get the water ready. As she walked towards the bathroom, with her daughter at her side, she turned to her grandson and said, "I'll be right back after a quick bath." Throughout the bath, she chatted with her helper. When done, they went back to her room, and she picked out a house gown from a stack, one of her favorites - a lavender floral print. Her helper gave her a hand to put it on.

What followed would change from an ordinary morning to not-an-ordinary morning for all the ones who love her so.

It was ten thirty in the morning by then. Sitting on the bed, with one arm in her gown and the other half in, she gently wavered to one side, towards her bed. Her daughter and grandson rushed to her room to respond to the helper's call. They cried and called out to her, begging her to say something. They hugged her tightly, and then she leaned over to her daughter's arms and took in her final breath.

A life well lived. Ninety-three years of blessings shared by many. Now we will have to go on with the memories. We thank God for giving her to us for this long to love and cherish.

My precious mother was so blessed to be a blessing to anyone who knew her. She was fortunate to spend the last several months of her life with her younger daughter and family. With a son-in-law who loved her like his own mother and a grandson and his wife, all of whom were so loving, respectful, and attentive, she was well cared for until she took her last breath. December 4, 2016, four months to the date from her ninety-third birthday of August 4, 2016.

As for me, that Saturday was a happy Saturday. Grandchildren were home, having slept over on Friday night. As they played around, I made my usual phone call to Ammachy. As we talked, she heard the little ones in the background. I asked them to say hello to "India Ammachy" as they referred to her. They each came and said, "Hi, Ammachy" into the phone. I could tell her heart was full hearing their sweet voices. She said she felt "a little tired but not sick or any-thing" during the conversation. Then we talked a little longer than usual and gave the phone to Valsa, my sister, so we could talk and said goodbye.

The day went on, happy and pleasant. Mar Thoma Church car-olers came in the evening. Tisha and Anupam came by to pick up the children. Our entire family of eight, including Tikku, enjoyed the carols. After Tisha and her family and the carolers left, I went to bed.

There was a sense of uneasiness as my head hit the pillow, won-dering how Ammachy was feeling. I thought of calling her to check, but I remembered her saying she "didn't feel sick or anything." So I thought I'd call her in the morning.

Then, around midnight, the phone rang. I saw the number and picked it up with trembling hands to hear Tittu, my nephew's heart-breaking sobs and the words, "Kumari Aunty, our Ammachy's gone!"

My world crumbled to pieces. I had to gather myself to tell the family here and plan to make that lonely, long trip home to see her off.

In the hours between the trip, the family here was by my side, grieving with me, helping with ticket arrangements, packing, hugging, crying, and fondly remembering her.

I don't know how I drove to church for the 7:30 a.m. service. I knew I was serving that day. It must have been her sense of duty and her will of steel or the sacrificial giving of my beloved Papa, who had been gone for twenty years before her.

Taking the flight alone from RDU to Trivandrum via Abu Dhabi is something that to this day feels so surreal.

Meeting the family at the airport in Trivandrum, the ride to their home with Tittu and Kochaniyan, walking into their living room to see the broken-hearted little sister, in whose shoulder she took her last breath, seeing the empty sofa where she used to sit and the empty bed where I last slept with her, and she gently stroked my face and hugged me tight on the night before my return to the US.

Consoling each other that we'll see each other "next year in January."

But to my utter heartbreak, December 4 came crashing down before January.

All that followed—the trip to the hospital mortuary with the heartbroken little brother and Tittu, seeing her lifeless body with a calm smile still frozen on her face, dressing her up in her favorite saree and blouse, the ride back home with her in the coffin…it all seemed like something out of a sad storybook.

The sendoff prayer by Bishop Barnabas and the local achens, Jesmy's heartbreaking cry as the rest of us left to take Ammachy back home to Edanad. Jesmy had to stay back due to being on bed rest for pregnancy-related reasons.

Staying up with Ammachy in the drawing room of Monchayan's home all night, singing and praying at her side as the day broke and people streamed in to see her one final time, the crowd who came to pay their respects to her as she waited in the pandal outside, and the final ride with her to the church.

Her beloved church where she worshiped for fifty plus years, served in the women's fellowship, sang in the choir into her seventies, and where our beloved papa's mortal remains rest. Her favorite Bishop Thimotheos and several achens officiated the service—and just like that on the tenth day of December 2016, we saw her face one last time.

And she joined our beloved papa in their joint resting place.

Not a day passes by that they are not remembered in prayers of gratitude.

I also ask for forgiveness if I ever knowingly or unknowingly hurt them in any way.

I am forever grateful for the blessing of being their daughter.

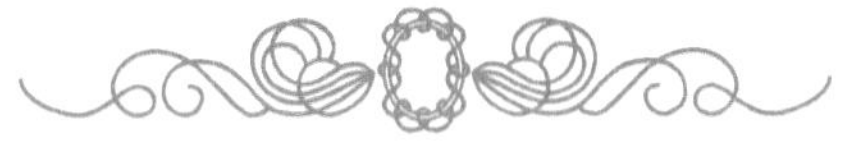

Who Inspires You?

Who inspires me? The answer is in plural. My God and the faith of my forefathers (and foremothers). Then a whole host of people. My everyday heroes. Family, friends, colleagues, my patients and their families, random people doing their daily work, my church family, all of them. Everyone doing their best under all kinds of circumstances. They inspire me. I marvel at their skills, their tenacity, their courage, and grace. Their kindness, humility, and empathy.

They cheer me on, let me lean on them, let me see my hidden strength, and even let me see my weaknesses. I am who I am and where I am because they cared, sometimes even unknowingly. I am forever grateful for their presence in my life. It is hard to list everyone, but I will try.

My beloved children Tikku and Tisha, and grandchildren Arjun, Krish, and Ava, their dad Anupam who inspires me to be a true practicing Christian. My precious parents and siblings.

The group of friends who are like family: Charlotte, Bavakutty, Valsa, Reema, Lillykutty, Ramani, Monie, Barb, Lisa, Judy, Billie, Andree, and Leslie. Beth, Erika, Sylvia, Selvi, Margaret, Betty, Faye.

My mentors Barney and Khalil. My forever friends from KMC: Omana, Darley, Sreedevi, Kanchana, Cisy, Hema, Leelu, Mithra, Kripa, Mohan, Sundaram, Thangam, Sathi, Shailaja, Mary, Sarala, Radha, and Lourdes.

All of them, in one way or another, in so many ways, have inspired me.

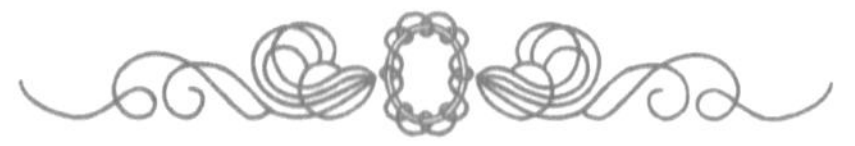

Life After Punnon
Home: The Quilt

Having spoken about my childhood home, life in the small island village where I grew up, and the loving family and home I left behind, it is now time to talk about life after Punnun home. I will refer to it as the *Quilt*—a collection of many shapes, prints, and sizes of delicate fabric, representing my life as an adult in a land that I never expected to settle down in and call home, all sewn together by a thread of many strands: faith, love, hope, joy, pain, regrets, defiance, bitter failures, and a few sweet successes.

A marriage that was never intended to be as he confessed to a group of couples at a recent gathering. During a game of "the secret of your success," where each couple shared how long they had been married, how they met, and the secret to their successful union, we revealed that we had been married for forty-nine years, had an arranged marriage, and met in my parents' home. Those were the easy answers. The couple before us shared their story, and then it was our turn. To my horror and shame, I heard his answer: "I always wanted to be a bachelor, but her brother begged me." When pressed for further explanation, all he could do was repeat the same lie: that he wanted to remain single, but my brother, his college mate, begged him to marry me!

They turned to me for my perspective. It was not my brother who intervened, but his own mother. She had been referred to my parents by a mutual friend. I was away at medical school when she visited my parents, saw several pictures of me, spent time with my parents, grew fond of them, and asked for a picture of me to send to her son and daughters in the United States. While waiting for their response, she continued to visit my parents and requested that they not promise me to anyone else but her. It took at least a week for letters to travel overseas—one week to get there and one week to return. She maintained the pressure. When she received a positive response from her son and daughters, she returned to my parents with the letter and asked them to agree not to make any commitments until her son arrived from the US and I returned from Mangalore for our respective vacations in two to three months.

During that time, she visited my parents frequently, sharing letters from her children and reminding them of their promise.

Three months later, we returned to our respective homes. Mother and a couple of relatives brought him home to my parents' house. We had a few minutes alone, and they asked him for his thoughts. He expressed his willingness to proceed with the wedding arrangements. When asked, I also agreed, although I expressed uncertainty about whether it meant I would be living in America. Mother reassured us that he had no plans to move to America, but rather intended to stay for a few years and then return to Kerala to "settle down."

Given those circumstances and the main reason I agreed to marry him—to be closer to my home, with his family's home just four or five miles away—I agreed as well. We were married two weeks later. So he was right; he may have felt pressured, not by my brother, but by his mother, who rained on his parade without knowing that he had wanted to remain a bachelor his whole life.

Against this backdrop, we began to build our family. One of us was fully committed to creating a family similar to yours—parents and at least four children, a short stay in America for post-graduation studies, and then returning to India with our family to "settle down" in our home, practice medicine, and raise children surrounded by grandparents and close to my parents, siblings, and their children. Life was meant to mirror the loving family life we had at Punnun Home. The other, however, had no interest in investing in a family and was fiercely independent and self-indulgent.

What followed was a story of many challenges for both of us. The one who wanted to remain single faced the difficulties of building a life contrary to his desires, while the one who longed for a replica of her childhood family struggled to balance a demanding medical career while holding onto traditional family values. Raised by two incredible parents—loving, hardworking, and gracious individuals who practiced selfless giving—I tried to give my best to my precious children. They were and still are my world. My faith in God sustained me through numerous storms. My shortcomings and limitations were numerous, and my best efforts often fell short. My children became victims of my imperfections. Yet, purely by the grace of God, they have become good-hearted individuals and responsible citizens in the roles they have been blessed with.

There are many beautiful patches of joy from their lives, as well as some ugly stains caused by their imperfections. As I look at this quilt with its many colors, shapes, and sizes, I find so much beauty in it despite the stains. I am grateful to God for the individuals they have become. I pray that God will watch over them and keep them safe, and that they will be bound together by a godly spirit of sibling love.

I am also thankful to God for the blessing of my wonderful grandchildren, and I pray that they will grow up to be good citizens. I hold them in my prayers always, seeking their spiritual, mental, emotional, and physical well-being. I also pray that my children will find peace in their hearts and that their souls will forgive me for the many shortcomings I have had.

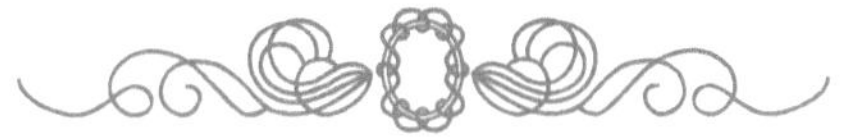

My Father's Kind Heart

He lived…I watched…I learned, in awe of my beloved father, my gold standard, for all the roles he played.

My heart sings in joy and gratitude for the blessing of being your daughter.

Always in my heart, in my prayers of gratitude.

My *papa*, till we meet again.

"Crane!" he exclaimed, using my pet name, as we gathered around the table for our evening coffee.

After a long and enjoyable day spent as a family, visiting the rubber estate and having lunch at our favorite local restaurant, we returned home to rest and take a nap. Coffee time after the nap was always a delightful moment to cherish our family bond, engaging in small talks and sharing stories.

During our ride back home, I had noticed a few white birds in the paddy field by the roadside. Since I was not very familiar with the English language at that young age, I turned to him, my papa, and asked him their name in English. He replied, "Oh! It slipped my mind momentarily. It's on the tip of my tongue, but I can't quite recall it. I'll let you know when I do."

And then he suddenly remembered, saying, "Crane! Those are the birds you inquired about!"

No question was ever considered too silly or unworthy of an answer in his eyes.

He was always attentive, deeply caring, respectful, loving, and devoted to us, his family. He gave his all, leaving no doubt about the depth of his commitment and love for us.

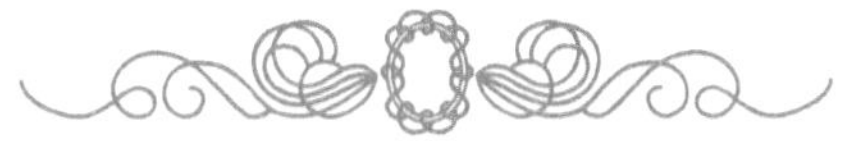

Cherished Memories of My Father

I hope he is smiling in heaven, my beloved father.

Today, as I "fixed" this beautiful twenty-five-year-old clock, a thoughtful gift from Stu, a sweet and kind friend from work, I couldn't help but think of him. Stu was a survivor of a horrendous auto accident. Despite her crushed body, her sturdy and stoic spirit remained intact. She was a kind and feisty individual who cared for our patients with great passion, her big heart shining through.

The clock resides in a room I don't frequent daily. However, today, while passing through, I noticed that it had stopped. I couldn't determine for how long.

My heart sank when I saw the dead, corroded AA battery inside. It needed to be fixed, I thought, though I wasn't sure if it was salvageable.

But then, a smile crossed my face as I remembered my precious father, the ultimate fixer-upper. I used to watch him in awe as he patiently and meticulously repaired little things.

I got to work, cleaning the crusty mess, and it cleaned up well. Filled with excitement, I inserted the battery, only to realize I had put it in the wrong way. Disappointment washed over me momentarily, but it quickly turned to joy when I repositioned the battery correctly and the clock started ticking again!

Today I smiled with immense pride over this small achievement, with two very special reasons behind it.

First, it reminded me that I am my father's prodigy.

Second, Stu's gift will continue to tick and keep time.

Indeed, it's the small things that matter. I am incredibly thankful for these beautiful memories.

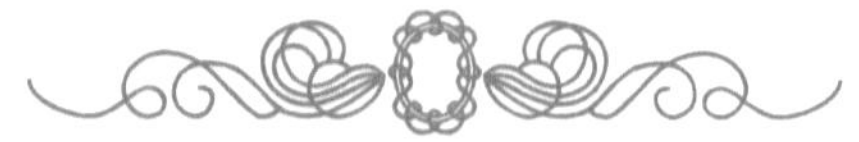

Cherished Memories
of My Mother

She had a deep love for flowers and a passion for sewing.

At the age of twenty-two, while expecting her first child among the four she would have, she turned to sewing as a way to combat morning sickness and keep her mind occupied. Taking a white sheet, she began embroidering intricate designs on all corners and in the center. She skillfully created flowers in various colors and shapes.

Her sewing talents extended beyond embroidery. She also lovingly crafted dresses and outfits for her children using her favorite Singer sewing machine.

In addition to her sewing, she cultivated a beautiful garden filled with roses, jasmine, marigolds, table roses, and many other flowers of vibrant colors and delightful fragrances.

I feel blessed to call her my mother.

I must apologize for not taking up either of your beloved hobbies. However, I am immensely proud to honor you with this humble gardenia from my own garden as it is the only flower I have.

I am eternally grateful and feel incredibly blessed that God chose both of you to be my beloved parents. I cannot think of one of you without thinking of the other. I am so blessed and so grateful.

I miss you both every single day.

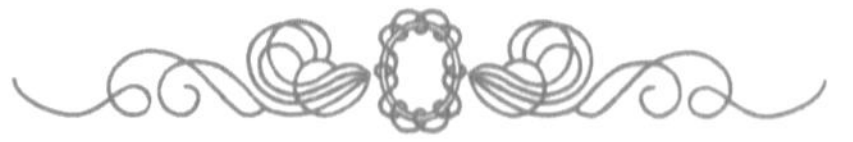

Celebrations Through Psalms

"The Lord is my Shepherd…" (Psalm 23).

This psalm has always been a favorite of mine, offering comfort and reassurance during times of worry or concern. Many years ago, I came across an open book with gilded edges displayed on an easel. On the left page, the psalm was written, and on the right page, there was an image of the Good Shepherd carrying a lost sheep, with a few anxious little sheep by his side. I purchased it and brought it home, placing it strategically where I could see it whenever I entered or left the house.

Every day, before leaving home, I would pause by this book, read the psalm, and say a special prayer for anyone I knew who had a specific need—whether it was related to physical or emotional health, work concerns, or relationship issues. I would also pray for each member of my family, addressing their individual needs. Lastly, I would ask for divine guidance as I fulfill the various roles entrusted to me in my life. There were times when I would personalize the prayer by replacing the pronouns with the names of those who required special intercession. Walking away, I would feel a deep sense of calm and comfort, knowing that the Good Shepherd had them covered.

This psalm, along with another favorite, Psalm 121, took on a greater significance when our first grandson, Arjun, was born to our daughter Tisha and her husband, Anupam, in January 2009. As I pondered a gift for Arjun on the day of his baptism, it struck me that the best gift would transcend time and trends. It should come from the heart, inspire him, and instill hope. That's when I combined these two favorite psalms and composed an original hymn, hoping that as he grows older, he will read and internalize the meaning of each verse, living a life of Christian faith and confidence. My intention was to envelop him in love and provide him with the tools to build a strong foundation that would make his parents proud.

Then, in May 2010, we were blessed with the arrival of his little brother, Krish. Filled with love and gratitude, we celebrated both their baptisms at St. Paul's Episcopal Church. With the assistance of Reverend Sally Harbold, I handed over my hymn to the choir directors, who kindly agreed to have it sung by the choir at both Arjun's and Krish's baptisms, which were a year apart.

In 2014, we were privileged to celebrate the baptism of our youngest grandchild, Ava. The choir's rendition of the music was exquisite, leaving their parents, grandparents, family, and friends in awe of its beauty.

Now, when I hear these psalms, they hold a new significance for me—one that is even more personal, comforting, and inspirational. It brings a smile to my face, knowing that my loved ones and I are safely embraced in the arms of the Good Shepherd.

> *Dear Lord, we express our gratitude for Your sacrifice on behalf of Your flock. Help us remember that Your goodness and mercy will accompany us wherever we go, in every aspect of our lives. We ask this in the name of Jesus. Amen!*

Psalm 121

1. I will lift up mine eyes unto the hills, from whence cometh my help.
2. My help cometh from the Lord, which made heaven and earth.
3. He will not suffer thy foot to be moved, he that keepeth thee will not slumber.
4. Behold he that keepeth Israel shall neither slumber nor sleep.
5. the Lord is thy keeper, the Lord is thy shade upon thy right hand.

6. The sun shall not smite thee by day, nor the moon by night.
7. The Lord shall preserve thee from all evil, he shall preserve thy soul.
8. The Lord shall preserve thy going out and thy coming in from this time forth and even for ever more.

The Lord Is My Shepherd
(Tune of "Blessed Assurance")

The Lord is my shepherd I shall not want
He is my keeper savior and friend
He restores my soul and leads me along
Streams of still waters pastures of green
The Lord is my shepherd I shall not want
He is my keeper savior and friend

(2)
Trials and temptations I shall not fear
Keeper of (Daniel/Jacob) He is my friend
I lift up my eyes and call on His name
Out pours His mercy, pardon and grace
The Lord is my shepherd I shall not want
He is my keeper savior and friend

(2)
His eyes watch over each step I take
My going out and my coming in
He holds my hands and leads me along
From this day forward and ever more
The Lord is my shepherd I shall not want
He is my keeper savior and friend (2)

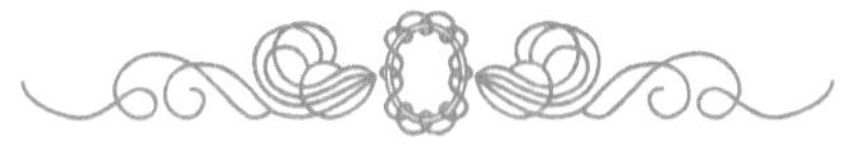

Remembering Some Proud Moments

Kumari Daniel

Class: PPC class of 1965.

Left KMC in '72 to continue house surgency at Kottayam

Married Chacko P. Verghese, MSc, bio-chemistry from Roosevelt University, Chicago, Illinois, in September '72. After completing house surgency, migrated to USA in November '73. Lived in Detroit, Michigan, till June '79.

Completed general psy-chiatry residency and fellow-ship in child psychiatry and moved to North Carolina in June '80 to get away from the brutal Michigan winters.

Took first job with the state of North Carolina as an attending psychiatrist in one of its four psychiatric hospitals.

Retired from state and county services after thirty-five years of holding both clinical, academic, and director roles in February 2015. Currently I do part-time consulting at a local hospital, covering ER and hospital consults. Chacko, who worked at Glaxo Wellcome, is also retired.

Blessed with a son, Tikku, in '74 and daughter in '79.

LIFELINER

Your Johnston Health News Source

JOHNSTON UNC HEALTH CARE

Feb. 4, 2015

NOTEWORTHY

Health Chats to focus on hearts
At the next Health Chats on Feb. 11, Dr. Benjamin Atkeson will talk about the advances of cardiology. The hour-long sessions will start at 11 a.m. in the auditorium of the Johnston Medical Mall and at 6 p.m. at The Clayton Center. To reserve a seat, register online at the Johnston Health website.

Need a scholarship?
The Johnston Health Volunteers Council is accepting applications now through April 15 for scholarships to students who are pursuing professions in health care.

Students are eligible if they live in Johnston or an adjacent county. They must have a grade point average of 3.0 or higher, and must demonstrate financial need. The council will also consider extra-curricular activities and work ethic.

Copies of the application form are available in the Volunteer Gift Shop. Also, the form can be downloaded from volunteers page on the Johnston Health website.

At-home sleep studies now available
The cardiology department at Johnston Health is now offering home sleep-testing services. The new device provides patients with the ability to be screened at home for obstructive sleep apnea. This is a one-night test, and set up for use of the device takes less than 10 minutes. Shelby Holt, director of cardiopulmonary services and sleep, says her department on Jan. 21 did its first home sleep test. "It's convenient, and best of all, patients can sleep in their own bed."

A gift to assist patients
The Johnston Health Foundation has received its first corporate gift for a fund aimed at removing some of the most basic obstacles to a patient's treatment and recovery. A $9,000 contribution from the Piedmont Natural Gas Foundation doubles the size of the newly established Johnston Health Patient Assistance Fund, which will begin disbursements system wide in February. Eligible expenses include medications and transportation to and from doctors' offices.

Please observe employee pharmacy hours
Need a refill, a new prescription or an over-the-counter item? Please drop off or pick up orders weekdays from 7 a.m. till 6 p.m.

Donna Dewberry, employee pharmacist, staffs from 8:30 a.m. till 5 p.m. An inpatient pharmacist covers the earlier and later hours, when inpatient orders will take priority over employee prescriptions.

New *prescriptions* that are considered to be urgent may be filled after hours. However, *OTC* requests will be filled only during weekday hours of operation. Urgent prescriptions include antibiotics, non-steroidal anti-inflammatory agents, corticosteroids, anti-diabetic agents, antiretrovirals, anticonvulsants, inhalers/inhalants, immunosuppressants, antiplatelets, antihypertensives (all categories), antivirals, antimigraine agents, and any other prescription deemed urgent by the pharmacist on-duty.

LifeLiner is published on the first and third Wednesdays by the Marketing and Community Relations Department

**Suzette Rodriguez......writer, editor
Erin Bailey...social media, website**

To submit news items, call 938-7103 or email srodriguez@johnstonhealth.org. Follow us on Facebook and Twitter.

GO RED FOR WOMEN!

Employees in cardiology wore red this week to show their support for women's heart health. From left to right are: Nicole Wellons, Whitney Anderson, Michelle Cook, Janet Evans and Renee King. Look for more photos on Johnston Health's website.

Raising awareness about heart disease

Did you know that heart disease accounts for one in three female deaths in the U.S. every year? It's the number one killer of women, says the American Heart Association, yet the disease is largely preventable. Unfortunately, 64 percent of the women who die suddenly of coronary heart disease have no previous symptoms, according to an AHA 2012 study.

You can help raise awareness about heart disease by wearing red on Friday. You can join in the Go Red campaign by snapping photos of co-workers in red. Send these to Erin Bailey, and she'll post them on Facebook. Also, pick up a heart-shared squeeze ball from one of the Go Red tables set up in the Smithfield and Clayton cafeterias, and enter the drawing for a prize. The squeeze balls will also be distributed to inpatients, and registrars will be distributing pins to outpatients.

Pearson named `HD of Year'

Marilyn R. Pearson, MD has been chosen as 2015 Health Director of the Year for her leadership and commitment to the health and wellbeing of Johnston County residents.

The North Carolina Association of Local Health Directors honored her on Jan. 21 during an awards luncheon in Raleigh.

Dr. Pearson began her career in the Johnston County Health Department. After seven years as a physician in the health clinics, she became health director and medical director. In that role, she supervises three physicians, five mid-level providers and other managerial support teams. She also oversees services provided in the adult, pediatric, epidemiology, maternity and family planning clinics.

In 2013, Pearson led the expansion of the health department with the addition of the behavioral health services division. Her work with other health partners to strengthen the medical safety net for the uninsured and underinsured was key to her being chosen for the award.

Pearson was also recognized for her service on several boards and committees, including the Living Well Partnership of Johnston County, the Johnston County Schools Agency Round Table, Partnership for Children, and Project Access of Johnston and Harnett Counties.

Behavioral Health recognized for making a difference

One of the busiest departments at Johnston Health is behavioral health, where the staff has taken on and embraced recent challenges wrought by the addition of state funding for indigent patients. What follows is director Shelly Malone's story of how the behavioral health team is excelling here at the hospital and reaching out to the community.

On Tuesday, CEO Chuck Elliott recognized the department for making a difference, and he praised the staff for its hard work and dedication.

People: Behavioral Health Services is known for being prepared for the various, and often unusual, psychiatric needs of all types of people from all walks of life. Because the needs can be diverse, the staff must be adept and diverse: calm, safe, respectful and therapeutic in response; refined in skill, expert in communication with folks who may not be able to express themselves accurately or well; creative in problem solving and efficient in use of limited resources. These folks are dedicated and love what they do, and they demonstrate this in the standard of quality in care they provide.

Quality: The team has consistently maintained an overall patient satisfaction score of greater than 90 percent for the past two years with a greater than 80 percent response rate. Scores for core measures have been commendable. We are proud that our departmental employee satisfaction ranks highly as well.

Growth: The team rose to the occasion when the state awarded us a contract, called Three Way Beds, to finance care for indigent patients. Our team was challenged with a 30 percent increase in volume and higher acuity. Indigent patients tend to be sicker with higher risks of co-morbidities and homelessness. Placements for these patients became an issue that demanded new processes and considerable time. The

The behavioral health department was recognized Tuesday with the Making A Difference award. From left, members of the team are: Kara Santucci, Nancy George, Randolph Reid, Jeffrey Williams, Cyril Reyno, Nasil Hussaini, Shelly Malone, Dr. Kumari Verghese, Dr. Henry Edmundson, Jeannette Lamm, Ashley Finch, Celeste Perri, Katharina Dewald, Elaine Howell, Morgan Heath and Julia Schindler. Sitting is Sophie, the therapy dog.

reporting requirements needed to maintain the state contract meant precision in patient care and accurate, elaborate documentation of our performance. During this same time, we also opened the new holding area in the emergency department. So our staff had to quickly adapt to providing a larger and more comprehensive service.

Value: Behavioral Health has made a huge financial turnaround. This past year, it began operating in the black for the first time. To do this, the staff has maintained high productivity by self-scheduling to provide the needed coverage.

Innovation: The team operates on the theory of "Pay it Forward," and we believe we get back what we give in life. We are grateful for every day that we can think clearly as we care for these dear patients who are unable to do so, either temporarily or permanently,

for whatever psychiatric diagnosis they bear. We are keenly aware that any one of us could suffer from mental illness, and we believe we should treat every patient the way we would want to be cared for.

We emphasize dignity and trust with our greatest therapeutic tools being listening and encouragement to enhance medication management. We train our team well in crisis intervention and therapeutic communication. Our hospital and the Johnston County Health Department provide medications to those who have no resources to buy their own. We feel obligated to provide for those who cannot do for themselves.

For the past three years, we have donated a WalMart gift card to the Smithfield Rescue Mission / Men's Homeless Shelter. We also contributed $200 to these services, which assist us with many of our patients in need.

Message from the CEO

Announcements

NEWS FLASH

Johnston Health

Best in the Region

Top 7 in NC

We learned recently that our performance for Hospital Acquired Conditions is the best in the region and one of the top 7 in North Carolina. This reflects our low infection rate and our patient safety measures.

HPSA Education

Coming in November

Watch your email and the newsletter for announcements about the HPSA Education Event. Marijka Lampard, President of HPSA Acumen Inc., will host an educational event about our approved HPSA designation for Johnston County and how we can all benefit from it.

Johnston Health Clayton

Watch your email and the newsletter for more information about the ribbon cutting celebration for the opening of our inpatient beds in Clayton. The date is January 10, 2015.

Dear Medical Staff,

I received a letter this week from Dr. Kumari Verghese telling me of her plans to retire by the end of the calendar year. Dr. Verghese is one of the most dedicated physicians I have gotten to know during my time here at Johnston Health and her work has been a major reason why our behavioral health unit has a strong reputation for the clinical care provided there. We all know the special talents of the physicians and staff that work with that patient population - hers set her apart. We will miss Dr. Verghese and her service not only to her patients but also to our organization. On the bright side she does plan to remain on staff so that she can come back on an "as needed" basis. We congratulate Dr. Verghese on reaching this stage of her career but we will miss her calming, compassionate, and collegial manner. We wish her the best.

Sincerely,

Chuck Elliott,

CEO & President

Financial Information

Financial Information YTD (June)	FY 2014	FY 2013	Change
EBIDA	16,518,674	16,591,797	- 0%
Net Income	5,507,023	2,592,429	112%
Admissions	5,894	6,100	- 3%
LOS	4.06	3.54	- 15%
Medicare Case Mix	1.48	1.44	3%
Total Surgical Cases	4,803	4,999	- 4%

Comments or ideas about the newsletter?
Email us: msoffice@johnstonhealth.org
or call (919) 938-7153.

www.JohnstonHealth.org

Health Chats
SEASONAL SPEAKER SERIES
BY THE JOHNSTON HEALTH MEDICAL STAFF
July 17, 2013 | 11:00am - 12:00pm
Johnston Medical Mall Auditorium

Behavioral Health Services In Your Community:
When, Where and How To Get Help

Presented By: Kumari D. Verghese, MD

Join Dr. Verghese as she discusses where and how to get help for yourself or a loved one who may be experiencing depression, mood swings, anger problems, substance abuse, or other mental health issues.

Speaker Bio
Kumari Verghese, MD, is a medical graduate of Kasturba Medical College, Mangalore, Mysore University, India. She completed her internship at Kottayam Medical College, Kerala University, India. After finishing a residency in adult psychiatry at Henry Ford Hospital in Detroit, Mich., she did a fellowship in child psychiatry and an advanced fellowship in infant, liaison and administrative psychiatry at the Fairlawn Center in Pontiac, Mich. Dr. Verghese has been practicing public sector psychiatry since 1980, starting with her services at John Umstead Hospital in Butner where she directed the dementia unit for several years. She then joined Dorothea Dix Hospital as the chief of service of the gero psychiatry unit, and now serves as the medical director for both Johnston County Mental Health Center and for behavioral health services at Johnston Health.

Upcoming Seasonal Health Chats
October 16, 2013
January 15, 2014
(Topics and speakers TBD)

Visit JohnstonHealth.org to register.
Johnston Medical Mall
514 N. Bright Leaf Blvd.
919-938-7186

JOHNSTON HEALTH

FREE! Behavioral Health Seminar!
Dr. Kumari Verghese
Health Chats
SEASONAL SPEAKER SERIES
BY THE JOHNSTON HEALTH MEDICAL STAFF
July 17
11:00AM
Register Online · www.johnstonhealth.org
InterState
07/07/2013

How Did We Decide How Many Children to Have?

Growing up with three siblings and many cousins in a loving family, I always knew that I wanted to have several children when I got married. As we embarked on our married life together in a new and foreign country, we faced numerous challenges. However, there was never any doubt in my mind about wanting to have children and how many. It was expected to be the natural course of events, and indeed it happened. Forty weeks after my arrival in Michigan, we were blessed with a beautiful baby boy. The experience of motherhood left me in awe. I never knew I could love someone so completely and unconditionally. I longed to have another child soon so I could share the same love all over again.

Months turned into years, and I missed having a second child with all my heart. Our innocent and loving little boy wished and prayed for a sibling with all of his heart. In the fifth year of the heartache of not having another child, we decided to consult a specialist. The infertility specialist suggested medications to stimulate ovulation, but I chose to observe Lent and pray during the forty days. In the first week after Lent, our prayers were answered. Forty weeks later, we joyfully welcomed our beautiful baby girl into the world.

I treasured every moment of raising her alongside her big brother. As much as I loved being a mother and desired more children, my husband was content with our family of four. So, like many major life decisions I had to make, I settled for yet another second choice—to not try for a third or fourth child.

By the seventh year of our marriage, I had sadly become familiar with the pain of making second choices and turning life's lessons into sweet lemonade. This made me a fierce protector of my maternal role. I loved those children with a love like no other. My decisions, from choosing the medical specialty to pursue, to the setting in which to practice, to living alone and venturing into a completely unfamiliar practice setting temporarily to compensate for job and income loss due to their father's early retirement—all of these decisions were made to give them the best life I could provide.

Later, I would come to understand that my best was not sufficient, not for them or their father. Nevertheless, within my heart, I hold on to that fierce and delicate love—an affection unlike any other I have ever experienced—with every fiber of my being. *Mom!* The most endearing name I have ever been called. My humble and grateful heart will continue to love them as long as the good Lord allows it to beat.

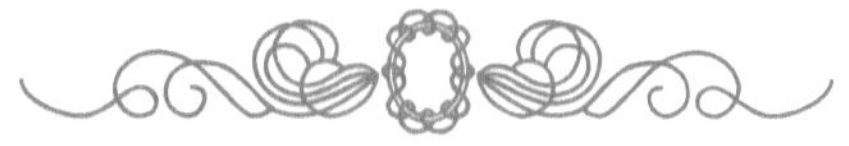

Reflections: Notes to My Children and Grandchildren

Looking back through the pages of my adult life, I ask myself: What are the most cherished stories of the roles I've been entrusted with? Without a doubt, I can say that motherhood and grandmotherhood top the list. Although I would never claim to be a perfect mother or a perfect grandmother, these two roles have brought me immense joy, pride, and fulfillment as a woman. In the presence of my children and grandchildren, I feel humbled and honored to be blessed with such an awe-inspiring gift.

To think that these little humans are intricately connected to my very being—they are an integral part of me in flesh, blood, and soul. While they didn't come packaged in beautiful boxes with instructions and owner's manuals, I instinctively knew it was love at first sight. I knew they would be the most cherished gifts I would ever receive. I knew they were here for me to love, teach, protect, and care for. Each of my children and grandchildren came into my life at different stages, naturally. Each one is incredibly precious and unique, holding a special place in my heart.

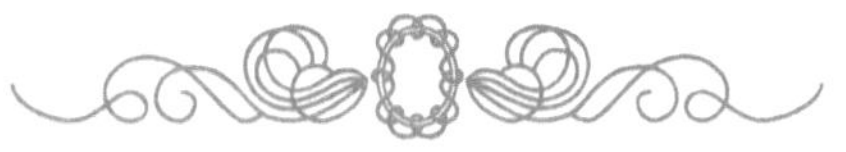

Between Dawn and Dusk

Most of our adult lives, from dawn to dusk, are spent away from our families, working alongside strangers who become friends, some even feeling more like family. Living my dream as a physician was the greatest blessing of my career, one that I will always be thankful for.

The choice of specialty, psychiatry, was entirely by chance and convenience. Psychiatry seemed to have less demanding on-call schedules, which I believed would allow me to better juggle family life and residency compared to other fields.

Initially, I had some reservations since I had limited exposure to psychiatry during medical school. However, with a ten-month-old infant, his care and well-being took priority over my desire to pursue the more demanding field of obstetrics and gynecology as my specialty.

After forty-five years of working in psychiatry in various clinical care and administrative settings, I feel truly gratified that it was God's will that led me to this field. I pray that I did my best to make a difference in the lives of the people I touched. I also pray for forgiveness from my children for not always being there for them when duty calls took priority over their precious needs.

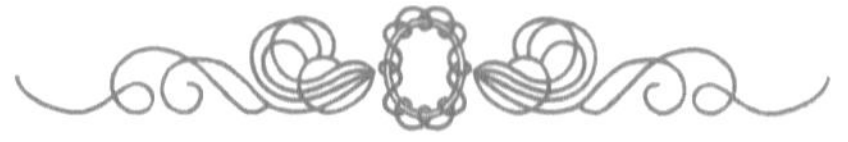

Field of Flowers

There is so much beauty in a field of flowers growing wild among the green grass. Flowers of different colors emerge from unrelated plants, creating a captivating sight. I often imagined my life to be like those wildflowers, growing in the vast field called life, blooming through various phases and experiences.

Looking back, many of the choices I made regarding my personal and professional life were made by chance rather than my deliberate choice. However, I can honestly say that deep faith and prayers guided my path, and it was by God's grace that I flourished where I was planted. At least, I hope so.

May my children and grandchildren be guided by faith, giving their best and becoming the best versions of themselves in all that life demands of them.

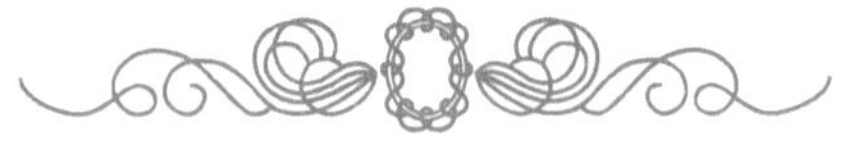

The Journey Called Life

A journey that began in a small village surrounded by the branches of a river in Kerala, India, would take me all the way to North Carolina, USA. From the southwest coast of India to the southeast coast of America, life in its various paths would teach me valuable lessons.

Growing up in an extended family with grandparents, parents, siblings, and cousins was an amazing experience. Wisdom, faith, love, patience, kindness, and graciousness were on full display, as well as stern discipline from the elders.

Life at the family home was filled with fun, love, peace, and joy. We prayed together, ate together, talked together, and laughed together. On Sundays, we worshipped together at the church where our ancestors had worshipped.

During holidays and special occasions, we would visit our relatives in other towns, and they would visit our home as well. Life was good.

The journey out of the beautiful, cozy island village began at the start of my second decade. My little sister and I were enrolled in a boarding school a few miles away from home. This school, founded by Christian missionaries, offered classes from elementary through high school for both residential students and local day scholars. We lived there throughout the school year and returned home for two short breaks during holidays, one for Onam (similar to a harvest festival) and the other for Christmas holidays. Our families visited us on weekends, and the summer break lasted for two months.

Though my sister was excited to go to boarding school with her big sister, parting was hard for her when the time came for us to leave home. However, her health issues took priority over the pain of separation and anxiety. I learned the value of sacrificial giving—giving my love and care to my little sister who looked up to me. In giving, I found courage for her sake and for my own.

After three challenging years, she returned to a local school, and I stayed the course and completed high school.

I cherish the blessings of the disciplined life I experienced there. The stern yet loving principal, Ms. Brooke Smith, all the teachers, the two devoted nuns, and the entire staff, as well as my classmates, seniors, and juniors—all contributed to shaping me. Starting and ending our days with morning and evening prayer in the chapel, and having access to the serene chapel for personal meditation during free time, allowed me to build upon the foundation of a faith-filled life that I witnessed at home.

Beautiful Edanad—the land in the middle—an island village surrounded by the River Pamba, near Chengannur, Kerala, India. Where my life journey started. In November 1973, I would leave my home here to start married life in the USA.

Spring in Apex, North Carolina (2020), where I would spend retired life

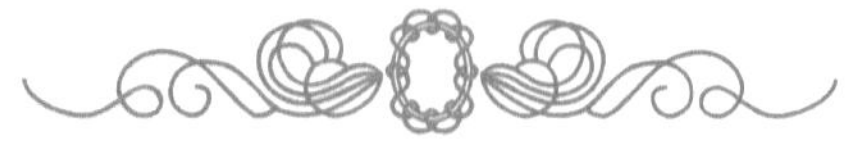

Out of Sight, Not Out of Heart

Some people come into your life and leave an indelible impression on your heart. Whether they are physically distant or gone too soon, their presence is felt as strongly as when you were living life side by side. I have been blessed to have some very special people like that in my life.

Here, I want to celebrate the latter group who, along with fond memories, bring on a gnawing ache just to have us sit side by side, ride together, or simply pick up the phone and say, "Hi, how are you? Want to drop by or meet for a cup of coffee?"

The first time I experienced the pain of losing a friend was when my best friend from middle school, Cisy, passed away due to breast cancer. We met while we were both in sixth grade, attending boarding school away from home. In just a few short days, we connected deeply. We shared the same ideals and dreams, had the same temperament, and had a similar zest for learning. We also enjoyed similar extracurricular activities like reading, singing, and dancing.

After leaving high school, we went to different colleges. I joined medical school a year into undergrad, and Cisy joined two years later after completing her undergraduate course, at the same medical school.

Though we were apart for four years and kept in touch through letters, we were ecstatic to pick up where we left off. After graduating from medical school, we parted ways again, with Cisy moving to the Middle East with her husband and me moving to the USA with my husband.

As always, we continued our friendship in all the years that followed, through letters, and met only once in 1983 when we both happened to be in Kerala on vacation at the same time. We were so excited to catch up in person after over a decade that we forgot to even take a picture together. However, we didn't forget to take one of our cute little daughters.

Then another decade later, she passed away. It broke my heart. My best friend of over three decades—a sensitive, kind, sweet, loving, gentle, and beautiful soul—was gone from this earth.

Her mother and I stayed in touch for many years.

As I grieved the loss of my dear friend, I also began to learn how to grieve and find peace in cherished memories.

Though not present in my life, Cisy's presence in memories remains vivid in my heart. Not long after the loss of Cisy, Baby Chechi, my friend from medical school who was two years my senior and felt like an older sister, also passed away from breast cancer. My family and I had just visited her family in Malaysia on our way back to the US from Kerala. I grieved for her as I would for a dear family member. Then I remembered all the kind and sisterly ways she cared for me and turned my sadness into joy for having had her presence in my life.

Another friend and classmate, Kanchana, who had lost both her parents before joining college, was more like a little sister to me. She even came home to spend an entire summer vacation with my family to experience family life again. It was touching to see how she embraced it all. After medical school, she married one of our classmates, and they practiced in Kerala while I was in the USA. She was the most selfless and kind-hearted person I ever knew, to the extent that she neglected her own physical health. Then, a few years ago, she passed away due to complications from poorly controlled diabetes. Not a day goes by without thinking of her. Her husband, Sundaram, remains as close a friend as she had been.

My dearest friend, Leealmma, whom I called Leelu, shared the worst pain I endured during the last years of our medical school life. We both experienced the pain of losing siblings, breakups with our first true loves, and settling for second choices. Despite living continents apart, we were able to maintain our strong bond throughout the years, sharing both good news and bad, tears and joy, until the last day of her life in August 2020. Even as she drifted into drowsiness from liver failure due to cancer, we were able to talk and see each other via video calls. She even made me sing an old hymn sung at funerals just a few days before taking her last breath.

The most unexpected heartbreak came from a chance encounter with a friend on Facebook. Rob, my favorite pharmaceutical representative, whom I had lost touch with since leaving John Umstead Hospital in 1995, had an uncommon last name that reminded me so much of my little brother, both in his mannerisms and appearance. After updating me on new products and asking for my feedback on how their products were working for my patients, we would indulge in sharing highlights of our family events. I mentioned how I had missed my little brother's wedding since I couldn't get vacation time as I had just moved to North Carolina a few months ago and started a new job. Rob shared pictures of his own family, including his young wife who was undergoing brain surgery for seizures, and I remember praying fervently for her. However, not long after in 1995, I took a new job in Rocky Mount, and we lost touch. But I never forgot Rob and his wife, Theresa, even though I had only seen her picture and had prayed for her.

Now, twenty-five years later, I came across a Facebook post from my friend Patty from the neighborhood. Patty had shared some beautiful pictures from her nephew's beach wedding over the weekend. In her comment, she mentioned how she missed her brother Rob but knew he was watching over Theresa, their sons Brad and Peter, and their son and his bride. My heart sank as I paid attention to the last names of Theresa, her son, the groom, and his brother. I could hardly see the letters on my phone screen as I typed a text to Patty, asking if her brother was a pharmaceutical representative. With a broken heart, I read her response about how Rob had passed away from non-Hodgkin's large B-cell lymphoma in October 1997, just a few months after my little brother and his family visited us from Dubai.

For years, I had wondered how my dear friend and his family were doing. This was not the answer I had expected, but at least I know he is with the Lord and that his family is doing well.

These five individuals, met at different stages of my life, each hold a special place in their own way. They are never forgotten. They have made me a better person for having had them in my life. Their kindness and goodness served as little flags, cheering me on through the trials I faced.

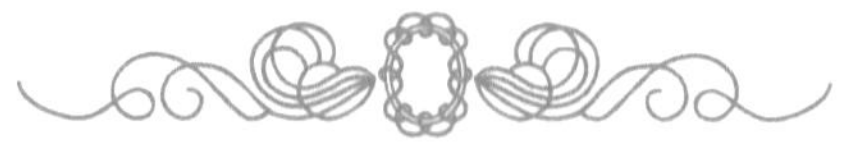

Grandchildren:
Precious Memories

Everyday moments that become cherished memories…
The first sleepover in a whole year.
I am grateful for God's amazing grace that kept us safe.
I am appreciative of the scientists and their team, the leadership, grounds team, the individuals who rolled up their sleeves to get

the vaccine, and all those who diligently washed their hands, wore masks, and practiced social distancing.

I am remembering with heartfelt sympathy those who will not have the opportunity to experience these moments again and hoping that their precious souls find eternal rest.

I am wishing comfort and peace to their loved ones. May they find solace in their faith and cherished memories.

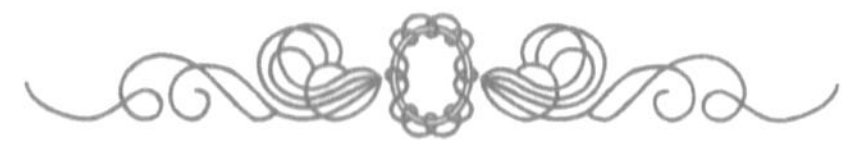

One Very Special
Thanksgiving and Birthday

Blessed Assurance

Blessed assurance, Jesus is mine!
Oh, what a foretaste of glory divine!
Heir of salvation, purchase of God,
Born of His Spirit, washed in His blood

Chorus:
This is my story, this is my song,
Praising my Savior all the day long;
This is my story, this is my song,
Praising my Savior all the day long.

Perfect submission, perfect delight,
Visions of rapture now burst on my sight;
Angels, descending, bring from above
Echoes of mercy, whispers of love.

Perfect submission, all is at rest,
I in my Savior am happy and blest,
Watching and waiting, looking above,
Filled with His goodness, lost in His love.

The year I learned the joy of simplicity and pure gratitude.

The year when the meal tasted as good as, or even better than ever, served from takeout containers instead of my bulky, yet beautiful serving dishes that we decided didn't need to be used.

There was no busyness, no rush. Just our small family of eight gathered around the table, set by our son.

Our daughter and her family picked up the food, walking in with not only the delicious meal but also birthday cards and flowers in the cutest vase that had the words "thankful, grateful, blessed" written on it. It was a truly blessed moment when I limped up to greet them.

Hugs were exchanged along with heartfelt "Happy birthday, Mom, Ammachy" (it was also my birthday).

While waiting for Dad/Appacha to get ready, I suggested that the children and I sing a song I had written for them, a combination of two of my favorite psalms, 23 and 121. This would give us a head start instead of waiting long for Appacha's usual brief blessing.

I told them that the song was to the tune of "Blessed Assurance" and sang it for them. We also read the touching story behind that hymn. Then we served ourselves and sat down to eat. To everyone's surprise, the turkey tasted better than ever, even for those who weren't fans of turkey.

The younger ones and adults took care of cleaning up while the seniors sat down and enjoyed watching them.

At the end of the day, I looked at those three little words written inside a heart and wondered if *blessed* is the cause or effect of the other two.

This year, more than ever, as I am still recovering and have had plenty of downtime to myself, I truly believe that there are countless blessings we take for granted, such as the most enjoyable quality time spent with loved ones, good health, peace of mind, and so much more.

Thanksgiving is more than just the meal, the elaborate feast. It is primarily about recognizing those blessings and expressing gratitude.

On the other hand, being thankful and grateful will also open our hearts to receive and experience countless blessings. The icing on the cake was what awaited us in the hallway before our daughter and her family left. Someone started singing "Happy Birthday," and everyone joined in. One by one, we exchanged warm wishes and hugs, and they began to walk out. Little Ava, the youngest, came back to give me one more huge hug. Then she whispered so sweetly and softly, "I can't wait for us to come back and stay" (all four of us, Arjun, Krish, and I had missed those sleepovers due to COVID and my back trouble).

I eagerly replied, "Me too." She smiled, a twinkle in her bright eyes, and said, "You know, we have a lot of no-school days coming up!" I responded, "Yes, sweetie, I know," and we hugged again, eagerly thinking about those "no-school days" and sleepovers, God willing.

The Lord Is My Shepherd
(A combination of Psalms 23 and 121,
written for my grandchildren)

The Lord is your shepherd, you shall not want
He is your keeper, savior, and friend
He restores your soul and leads you along
Streams of still waters, pastures of green

The Lord is your shepherd, you shall not want
He is your keeper, savior, and friend (2)

Trials and temptations you shall not fear
Keeper of children, he is your friend
Lift up your eyes and call on his name
Out pours his mercy, pardon, and grace

The Lord is your shepherd, you shall not want
He is your keeper, savior, and friend (2)

His eyes watch over each step you take
Your going out and your coming in

He takes your hand and leads you along
From this day forward and forevermore

The Lord is your shepherd, you shall not want
He is your keeper, savior, and friend (2)

(Sung to the tune of "Blessed Assurance")
Written by Kumari Verghese

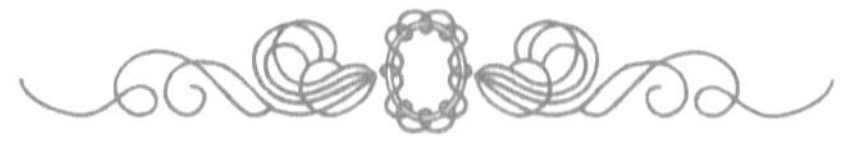

You Can Never Go Home Again?

I've heard it said, "You can never go back home again." I wonder if I'm an oddball or a sentimental old fool.

In the years since I left that beautiful island village and the precious family and home I left behind, exactly forty-eight years ago this week, I have revisited it a thousand times. Sometimes I took that long plane journey alone or with family, armed with pricey plane tickets, passports, and visas.

But more often, I ventured there alone with eyes closed, observing the clouds float by over blue skies, or witnessing a rainbow after a good downpour, or experiencing a beautiful sunrise or a bright moon in the dark of night. It came free of charge, with no bags to pack, and no passport to carry.

I simply opened the eyes of my heart wide, and there I was, at home with the people, family mealtimes, prayer times, and moments of relaxation in the front yard beneath the dark skies, with the moon and stars shining down on us as we talked, laughed, and reminisced about all the visits from families and friends, the celebrations, and the anticipation of more special events. I was there, living it all.

I could even catch a whiff of the fresh-bloomed jasmine flowers from the vine that wrapped around the wrought-iron arch over the front steps.

I could almost smell the gentle fragrance of the newly blossomed jasmine from the vine that enveloped the cast-iron arch at the gate.

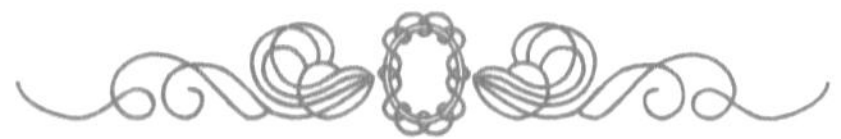

What Makes My Heart Smile and Eyes Close in Prayers

My precious grandchildren! Every time I think of them, my heart bursts with love, leaps with joy, and my eyes close in prayer. I thank God for blessing me to be their grandmother. I think of each of them with a love that I never knew a heart could feel. It is pure, intense, and entirely unselfish, wishing only the best for each of them. I pray for their health—physical, mental, emotional, spiritual, intellectual, and social. I pray for guidance, safety, and protection for them always and in all places.

My heart smiles as I recall special memories about them. Each grandchild is so unique and special in the way they share their love. We have made so many memories throughout the years—sleepovers, trips to the mall, bookstores, libraries, meals out, vacations to various attractions, and even our whole family trip to Kerala via Dubai to visit family. The time we have spent together and the memories we have made will always be cherished in my heart. Each time a memory comes up, my heart fills with pure love, joy, and gratitude.

I pray that they grow up to be kind, loving, and responsible citizens, and that they find happiness, contentment, safety, and prosperity. I pray that they will have a deep love for God, care for others, and always remain close to each other and their families. My heart will always pray for the best for each of my precious grandchildren and their families.

I also pray that their parents maintain close relationships with their own siblings and extended family, and that they are there for each other in times of need.

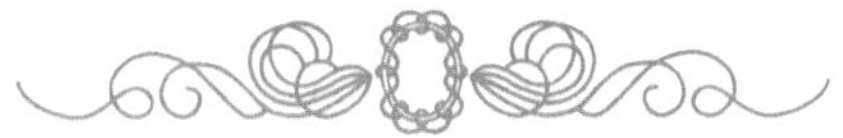

Things That Soothe My Soul

Amidst the haste, noise, pain, illnesses, unrest and all that ail our world, how refreshing it is to take in the calm and beauty of the rhythm of the nature.

Moonrise at sunset to full moon into the night.

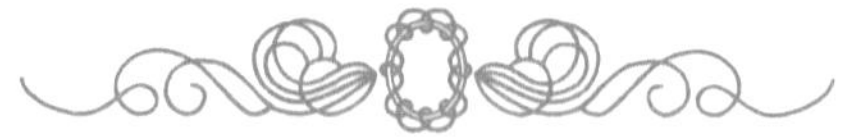

Looking Back Over
Forty-Nine Years

Yesterday marked the most consequential date in my life, forty-nine years ago (not this year, although it was eventful as our microwave oven unexpectedly stopped working and every place we checked seemed to have a back order). It was the day I embarked on adulthood—from the safety and comfort of the cozy, loving family nest, I was to begin a journey as a partner with someone I had met less than a fortnight ago. However, our families had the opportunity to get to know each other, and after our initial meeting at my parents' home, we both agreed to take this leap of faith.

Thus, we were married in the church, with the ceremony officiated by Rt. Rev. Dr. Yuhanon Mar Thoma Metropolitan (comparable to the role of the pope for Catholics as the head bishop of the Mar Thoma Church). I recognized the solemnity of the occasion. In the accompanying photo, you can see the Bishop holding an open book, Chacko examining the cover, and myself engrossed in the Bishop's advice (Chacko appears to be praying with his eyes closed, I believe). I still have that blue book of prayers and hymns, which I clutched tightly while the Bishop spoke.

Reflecting on the past, it feels similar to another significant event in September '72—commencing my internship after years of studying theory, participating in clinicals, and enduring written and practical exams. There would be subsequent roles and responsibilities such as residency, fellowship, attending, director, and so forth. However, with this "adulting" process, the lessons were learned by observing parents, elders, and other role models living out their lives rather than merely receiving lectures from teachers at a podium.

So in the forty-nine years that followed, these are what I learned:

- Rose bushes have thorns.
- There would be sunny days and cloudy days.
- Some clouds have beautiful silver linings.
- Rainy days may bring out beautiful rainbows.
- There can be streams in the desert.
- Detours on rough roads are for safety, and some may even have the best scenery.
- Broken hearts and joyful hearts can both bring out beautiful smiles (though for different reasons).
- Kindness, love, respect, dignity, hard work, honesty, and integrity are the foundation for peaceful coexistence.

- With God as the anchor and faith as the way, one doesn't need to travel alone in this journey called *life*.

There! My take on life.

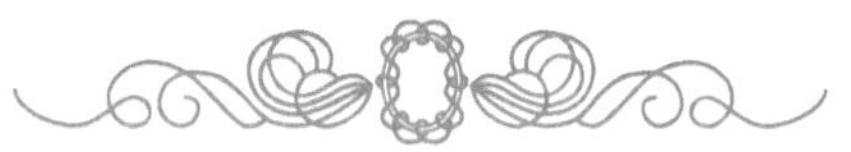

How Do I Thank You, Lord?

How can I adequately express my gratitude to You, Lord? You sent me on a detour, but along the way, You adorned the roadside with beautiful plants—even the thorny ones—and covered the thorny bushes with fragrant, stunning roses. I know it was all part of Your plan, to lead me to this distant land and bless me with two remarkable children, each arriving at the perfect time in my life.

I acknowledge that I have failed them and You as a mother, but You know I tried my best. There are consequences from my shortcomings, but I trust that You will watch over them because You are a loving, caring, merciful, and just God. You know that I love them with a love like no other. I wish them happiness, health, peace, and all Your amazing blessings. Thank You for holding them in the palm of your hands, shielding and guiding them through their life's journeys. May they lead virtuous lives that are pleasing in Your sight.

I also thank You for the gift of Anupam and the three incredible grandchildren, each uniquely special in their own ways. You know how my heart overflows with joy and gratitude when I hear them call me *Ammachy*, just as it does when I hear *Mom*. I pray that they may live happy, healthy, and virtuous lives, and that You will protect, guide, and bless them. I trust that You will provide for them as You do for Your precious children.

So how can I thank You for choosing me and entrusting me with these precious children—two of whom I gave birth to and one who joined our family by Your will? How can I thank You for blessing me with these three incredible individuals? There are not enough words to fully convey the depth of my gratitude. But on bended knees, with folded hands and a humble heart, I say thank You for honoring Your humble servant. Among all the women in this world, at those appointed times, You chose this woman, who grew up in a village and became a city-dweller, to raise and love these children and grandchildren.

Your kindness and grace in entrusting them to my care fill my heart with songs of joy and gratitude. I feel humbled and honored knowing that, just as You chose imperfect individuals during Your time on earth to carry out Your great works, You have big plans for them too. Thank You for assuring me of that.

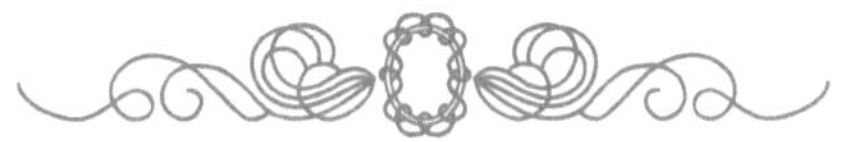

Have I Served You Well, Lord?

Almost six weeks into the new year and three days into this year, I take a moment to reflect on my sixty-seven years of life and pose this question to my Creator. As You intentionally and wonderfully created each of us and placed us on this earth, You assigned us numerous roles to fulfill. Looking ahead to the next phase of my life, which involves stepping back from the most visible public role I played as a physician for forty years, and anticipating the inevitable gaps in my personal life that will arise along the way, I wonder and ask, "Have I served You well, Lord?"

For it was in the faces of my parents, grandparents, siblings, uncles, aunts, cousins, husband, children, grandchildren, nieces, nephews, various in-laws, teachers, mentors, colleagues, teammates, patients and their families, preachers and ministers, friends, and those friends who feel more like family, that I found you. Thank You for always being there and showing me the way. I am aware that I have fallen short in many of these roles by not giving my best, but I hope that I made a sincere effort.

As I embark on this new year and the new phase of my life, I pray that the next few years, however many more You have in store for me, will be ones in which I can make it up to You and ask once again, "Have I served You well, Lord?" And may Your affirmation be evident through the faces of the individuals You have placed in my life.

Note: Reflections from January 2015 as I retire from full-time practice, only to return two months later and work part-time in different settings until full retirement five years later.

Johnston Health's Behavioral Health Services Staff

Extra Thoughts:

Inside this treasure chest you will find a collection of little gems, treasures collected by the author over seven decades. This is a bird's eye view into the life of a little girl who chose to trust the wisdom of her beloved parents and left home at a young age of little over ten years old to attend a boarding school. Though leaving the comfort and safety of her loving family was hard, she knew that her parents meant the best for her, and the best sounded like a treasure to cherish.

Building on a strong foundation based on Christian family values instilled in her by her parents, grandparents, and extended family, she will embark on her life journey. As she navigated through the many waters of life, she came across an abundance of gems which she tossed into a large chest.

She picked a few random ones and placed them in this small treasure chest for show and tell for any who might like to view them at their leisure. May these tokens touch a few hearts and put a smile on some faces.

9 798889 043975 8